PROJECT AIR FORCE

An Assessment of Options for Increasing Gender Integration in Air Force Basic Military Training

Agnes Gereben Schaefer, Darrell D. Jones, Andrew M. Naber, Thomas Goughnour, Nelson Lim

Prepared for the United States Air Force

For more information on this publication, visit www.rand.org/t/RR1795

Library of Congress Cataloging-in-Publication Data is available for this publication.
ISBN: 978-0-8330-9723-1

Published by the RAND Corporation, Santa Monica, Calif.
© Copyright 2018 RAND Corporation
RAND® is a registered trademark.

Support RAND

Make a tax-deductible charitable contribution at
www.rand.org/giving/contribute

www.rand.org

Preface

Currently, men and women in U.S. Air Force (USAF) Basic Military Training (BMT) sleep in gender-segregated flights; some training is gender-segregated, and some is gender-integrated. The USAF is currently reevaluating the degree of gender-integrated training (GIT) in BMT and asked the RAND Corporation to conduct an assessment of ways to increase GIT in BMT. This study consisted of five tasks:

1. reviewing the historical rationale for the degree of GIT in BMT and associated training outcomes
2. comparing USAF BMT with that of sister services
3. developing a range of options to incrementally and fully gender integrate USAF BMT
4. providing a comparative analysis of selected alternatives for gender-integrated BMT, including a cost analysis of the alternatives
5. developing an implementation monitoring framework and documenting findings and recommendations.

This report documents the findings from this study. It identifies five options for increasing GIT in BMT and assesses each option against a range of criteria, including:

- the degree to which GIT reflects working and housing conditions in the operational USAF
- the degree of integration across flights and trainees
- the impact on BMT training
- the impact on current military training instructor models
- the impact on BMT scheduling
- the impact on BMT facilities
- the impact on BMT information technology systems
- the implementation timeline
- the associated costs.

The report also identifies specific strategies to foster GIT implementation and presents a framework for monitoring GIT implementation over time.

The research reported here was commissioned by the commander of Second Air Force and was conducted within the Manpower, Personnel, and Training Program of RAND Project AIR FORCE.

RAND Project AIR FORCE

RAND Project AIR FORCE (PAF), a division of the RAND Corporation, is the U.S. Air Force's federally funded research and development center for studies and analyses. PAF provides the Air Force with independent analyses of policy alternatives affecting the development, employment, combat readiness, and support of current and future air, space, and cyber forces. Research is conducted in four programs: Force Modernization and Employment; Manpower, Personnel, and Training; Resource Management; and Strategy and Doctrine. The research reported here was prepared under contract FA7014-06-C-0001.

Additional information about PAF is available on our website:
http://www.rand.org/paf/

This report documents work originally shared with the U.S. Air Force incrementally in several briefings during fall 2015 and spring/summer 2016.

Table of Contents

Figures

Tables

Summary

Currently, men and women in U.S. Air Force (USAF) Basic Military Training (BMT) train and sleep in gender-segregated flights of 42 to 52 trainees. Recently, USAF leadership has become concerned that current levels of gender-integrated training (GIT) in BMT do not reflect integrated working conditions in the operational USAF—especially now that all positions in the USAF are open to women. USAF leadership is also concerned that current levels of GIT do not accurately represent to new trainees or to the public that diversity is a USAF priority. It is within this context that the USAF asked the RAND Corporation to assess ways to increase GIT in BMT.

This study consisted of five tasks:

1. reviewing the historical rationale for the degree of GIT in BMT and associated training outcomes
2. comparing USAF BMT with that of its sister services
3. developing a range of options to incrementally and fully gender integrate USAF BMT
4. providing a comparative analysis of selected alternatives for gender-integrated BMT, including a cost analysis of the alternatives
5. developing an implementation monitoring framework and documenting findings and recommendations.

Current State of Air Force BMT

As of September 30, 2016, women comprised 19 percent of USAF personnel and 19 percent of the enlisted corps ("U.S. Air Force Almanac 2017," 2017). BMT staff does not know how many men and women will arrive during any particular week, and the number of incoming women varies, making it difficult to plan and assign trainees to male and female flights ahead of time.[1] Two military training instructors (MTIs) oversee the training of each BMT flight. Female flights are required to have at least one female MTI, but both male and female trainees can have an MTI of the opposite gender. Male and female sleeping bays are located in the same dormitory building; some floors have female bays, while other floors are all male. Two flights are paired together so that they can conduct the same types of training activities at the same time. Female flights ("sister flights") are always paired with male flights ("brother flights"); due to the lower numbers of female flights, many male flights are paired with other male flights.

Despite this pairing, much of BMT training is what we term "same place and same time"— male and female flights carry out the same training activities at the same place and same time, but trainees are often not afforded the opportunity to interact across flights. Some examples of

---

[1] As part of this study, we analyzed 173 incoming classes from October 1, 2012, to March 28, 2016. Over that time,

these "same place and same time" activities include classroom training, some physical training (PT) activities, some inspections, training in the sleeping bays, and "instructor time" (when MTIs meet with their flights to discuss different topics). During other activities, such as the BMT capstone exercise—the Basic Expeditionary Airman Skills Training (BEAST)—men and women work together in integrated teams. Until 2015, the BMT Airmen's Run, Coin Ceremony, and graduation parade were also conducted in separate male and female flights. With the introduction of gender-integrated "Heritage Flights," male and female airmen now reorganize during their last week of training from gender-segregated squadron training flights into gender-integrated flights composed by career field.

Ways to Enable Full Gender Integration in BMT

To fully integrate BMT would require that incoming female trainees be assigned across all training flights. Either BMT staff would need to know ahead of time how many female trainees would arrive at BMT each week, or female trainees would need to be assigned to training flights after all trainees had arrived at BMT and the total number of women could be determined. Since the number of BMT slots is driven by the number of USAF technical training seats available and it is difficult to know how many women will actually arrive at BMT during any particular week, assigning trainees to flights ahead of time will likely continue to be impossible.

Another way to fully integrate BMT is to identify the total number of women in the incoming class after all trainees have arrived and then divide them across all flights.[2] One way to do this is by establishing a "processing flight," a temporary flight to which trainees would be assigned when they arrive at BMT. The USAF is the only service not to use processing flights at the beginning of basic training. Trainees would be assigned to a processing flight for the sole purpose of taking care of all of their in-processing activities (e.g., medical appointments, clothing issue, haircuts). When in-processing is complete, trainees would then be reassigned to their training flights. The concept of a processing flight could be incorporated into any of the GIT options discussed in this report.

Another way to enable full integration is to move to a MTI team model, which would facilitate greater communication and coordination across MTIs so that they can better manage the shift between gender-segregated sleeping bays to GIT flights. The 737th Training Group (TRG) has already proposed such a model. This model would provide more leadership opportunities for MTIs and more mentors to trainees. The net difference between the current and proposed MTI models is an increase of two instructor supervisors for each squadron.[3] These

---

[2] As part of this study, RAND developed a flight optimization model that can help the USAF determine the optimal proportion of men and women across flights, given the size of the incoming class; see Appendix D.

[3] The current model has one instructor for each of the four flights for a total of four instructors; the proposed model has two instructors for each of the three flights for a total of six instructors; therefore, the net increase is two instructors.

changes would apply to each of the six training squadrons; therefore, the total net difference is an increase of twelve instructor supervisors. Several of the options examined in this report include this new MTI team model.

RAND recommends that the USAF continue to explore ways to ensure a steady flow of female trainees to BMT and to consider establishing processing flights as a means to enable full gender integration in the long term. In the meantime, there are other options for substantially increasing GIT in BMT on a shorter timeline and with fewer major changes and costs. This report focuses on five such options.

Options for Increasing GIT and Associated Costs

After conducting a literature review, visiting USAF BMT, and visiting the enlisted basic training locations of the other services and USAF officer training programs, RAND identified five options for increasing GIT in BMT.

1. Integrate select training activities.
2. Integrate flights after trainees fall out from sleeping bays (50 percent men/50 percent women).
3. Integrate flights in the sleeping bays after morning hygiene (50 percent men/50 percent women).
4. Integrate as many flights as possible with 75 percent men/25 percent women (75/25 option).
5. Integrate sleeping bays.

These options could be pursued in isolation from one another, or they could be pursued sequentially through a phased approach that could ultimately lead to full integration of all flights. We present an overview of each of these options below.

Option One: Integrate Select Training Activities

There are opportunities to increase GIT in BMT without changing the way the USAF assigns trainees to gender-segregated bays and flights. For instance, many same place and same time training activities could be integrated without changing the current structure and composition of training flights and without impacting the current BMT schedule. Classroom instruction, some PT, drill, and visits to the dining facility are examples of training events and activities that offer opportunities to increase GIT. This option would not make fundamental changes to BMT, and of all the options, it would increase GIT the least. This option would also be the least disruptive to BMT scheduling and have the shortest timeline.

Option Two: Integrate Flights 50/50 After Fall Out From Sleeping Bays

The second option would require a few more changes to current BMT policies and procedures than the first option, but it would have a significant impact on increasing GIT. This option would retain the current BMT sleeping arrangements in the bays, in which bays are occupied by all-male or all-female flights. However, under this second option, after the trainees fall out for training in the morning, half of the men from one bay would combine with half of the women from another bay to form one GIT flight (half the flight would be men, half women).

This option would allow more trainees to experience GIT than the current BMT model, but because the limited number of female trainees would be integrated into training flights at high proportions (50 percent), not all training flights could be integrated—there are simply not enough female trainees to populate all training flights at 50 percent. Therefore, most male trainees would continue to train in all-male training flights. Fewer trainees and flights would be integrated under this option than under Option Four.

This option would fundamentally change the way training is conducted in BMT by creating a unique and new group dynamic. In essence, each trainee becomes part of two different groups: the group where he or she sleeps and the flight where he or she trains. This will require more coordination across MTIs and a new, team-based model of instruction, such as the 737th TRG MTI model discussed above.

Option Three: Integrate Flights 50/50 in Sleeping Bays After Morning Hygiene

The third option is similar to Option Two, with an important difference. Under this option, men and women would still sleep in separate bays. However, after trainees conduct "morning hygiene," in which they brush their teeth and get dressed, brother and sister flights would integrate while they are in the bays (rather than on the drill pad, as in Option Two). Like Option Two, this option would allow more trainees to experience GIT than under the current BMT model, but not all training flights could be gender-integrated. Fewer trainees and flights would be integrated under this option than under Option Four.

Like Option Two, this option would retain current sleeping policies and procedures. Therefore, trainees would be members of a gender-segregated sleeping bay group and a gender-integrated training flight. However, this option would allow training and mentoring activities (e.g., counseling, inspections) to continue to be conducted in the sleeping bays, as they are now. This is an important point, as many MTIs believe that training and mentoring time in the sleeping bays is pivotal to a trainee's transformation to an airman. This option would also require a team-based MTI model of instruction in order to increase coordination across MTIs.

Option Four: Integrate as Many Flights as Possible with 25 Percent Women (75/25 Option)

We specifically included this option because it was proposed by the 737th TRG as a means to increase GIT. This option is similar to Option Two in that it would retain the current BMT gender-segregated sleeping bays, and trainees would fall out and form integrated training flights. However, under this option, after the trainees fall out for training in the morning, they intermix and form GIT flights that are 75 percent male and 25 percent female.[4] Trainees would then conduct the day's training activities in these integrated training flights. This option would allow training and mentoring activities to continue to be conducted in the sleeping bays as they are now.

This option would allow more trainees to experience GIT than the previous options, and the male-to-female representation in flights in this option is more reflective of the USAF as a whole. Like Options Two and Three, trainees would be members of the group in their sleeping bay and the flight they train with. Therefore, like Options Two and Three, this option would also require a new, team-based MTI model of instruction.

Option Five: Integrate Sleeping Bays

This option represents the most integrated of the five options. With relatively minor modifications to sleeping bays, male and female trainees could participate, side-by-side, in all aspects of basic training, including where they sleep. The option to integrate sleeping bays is the most costly option and has the longest timeline due to facility impacts and changes. It is also important to note that Lackland AFB has already built four new airmen training complexes, and two more airmen training complexes are scheduled to come online in the next few years. Those new buildings are not currently configured to house gender-integrated flights and would need to be modified. The RAND team identified three options for modifying the bays in ways to allow them to be integrated:

1. 50/50 split of the sleeping bay without changing rooms
2. 50/50 split of the sleeping bay with changing rooms
3. 75/25 split of the sleeping bay with changing rooms.[5]

These different configurations are designed to work with the 50/50 options (flights with 50 percent men and 50 percent women) and the 75/25 option (flights with 75 percent men and 25 percent women).

---

[4] We did not include a 75/25 option for integrating in the bays because that would be logistically difficult.

[5] We did not include a 75/25 option without a changing room because that would be logistically difficult.

Summary of Assessment of GIT Options

Our analysis indicates that Option One is the least disruptive and expensive option. It does not involve any changes to sleeping bays, the current information technology (IT) system, or scheduling. Broadly speaking, Options Two, Three, and Four would have similar impacts on IT systems, scheduling, timelines for implementation, and costs. Options Two, Three, and Four would also require an MTI team model. Option Five is the most expensive option and has the longest timeline due to facility modifications. Table S.1 presents a summary of our assessment of the GIT options.

Table S.1. Summary of Assessment of BMT Gender-Integration Options

	Option One: Integrate Select Training Activities	Option Two: Integrate Flights 50/50 After Fall Out From Sleeping Bays	Option Three: Integrate Flights 50/50 in Sleeping Bays After Morning Hygiene	Option Four: Integrate as Many Flights as Possible with 25 Percent Women (75/25 Option)	Option Five: Integrate Sleeping Bays
Degree to which option reflects working and housing conditions in the operational USAF	• Reflects segregated sleeping conditions • Only somewhat reflects integrated working conditions	Most closely reflects segregated sleeping and integrated working conditions	• Does not reflect segregated sleeping and integrated working conditions	Most closely reflects USAF demographics	Does not reflect segregated sleeping and integrated working conditions
Degree of integration across flight and trainees	Smallest increase in GIT	• Fewer training flights could be gender-integrated than under Option Four • Flights that are integrated would experience very high levels of gender integration (50%)	• Fewer training flights could be gender-integrated than under Option Four • Flights that are integrated would experience very high levels of gender integration (50%)	Allows for larger proportion of flights and trainees to be integrated	Allows flights to be integrated all the time

	Option One: Integrate Select Training Activities	Option Two: Integrate Flights 50/50 After Fall Out From Sleeping Bays	Option Three: Integrate Flights 50/50 in Sleeping Bays After Morning Hygiene	Option Four: Integrate as Many Flights as Possible with 25 Percent Women (75/25 Option)	Option Five: Integrate Sleeping Bays
Impact on where BMT training occurs	• Maintains the current gender-segregated flight structure • Maintains training and mentoring in sleeping bays	• Training and mentoring activities could be maintained in in sleeping bays or moved to other venues • Members of the same bay would also be members of different training flights; this could potentially cause confusion • Could pose challenges for standardization of training	• Maintains training and mentoring time in sleeping bays • Members of the same bay would also be members of different training flights; this might cause confusion • Could pose challenges for standardization of training	• Training and mentoring activities could be maintained in in sleeping bays or moved to other venues • Members of the same bay would also be members of different training flights; this might cause confusion • Could pose challenges for standardization of training	Maintains training and mentoring time in sleeping bays
Impact on MTI model of instruction	No change to current MTI model of instruction	• MTI team model could provide trainees with more role models and mentors and MTIs with more leadership opportunities • MTI team model may require an adjustment period	• MTI team model could provide trainees with more role models and mentors and MTIs with more leadership opportunities • MTI team model may require an adjustment period	• MTI team model could provide trainees with more role models and mentors and MTIs with more leadership opportunities • MTI team model may require an adjustment period	• MTI team model could provide trainees with more role models and mentors and MTIs with more leadership opportunities • MTI team model may require an adjustment period
Impact on BMT scheduling	Does not require any scheduling or logistical changes	Could create more complex scheduling issues	Could create more complex scheduling issues	Could create more complex scheduling issues	Could create more complex scheduling issues
Impact on BMT facilities	No facilities modifications required	No facilities modifications required	No facilities modifications required	No facilities modifications required	Facilities modifications required

	Option One: Integrate Select Training Activities	Option Two: Integrate Flights 50/50 After Fall Out From Sleeping Bays	Option Three: Integrate Flights 50/50 in Sleeping Bays After Morning Hygiene	Option Four: Integrate as Many Flights as Possible with 25 Percent Women (75/25 Option)	Option Five: Integrate Sleeping Bays
Impact on BMT IT Systems	Does not require any scheduling or logistical changes	Requires change to IT systems used to assign and track trainees	Requires change to IT systems used to assign and track trainees	Requires change to IT systems used to assign and track trainees	Requires change to IT systems used to assign and track trainees
Timeline for implementation	Shortest	Medium-term	Medium-term	Medium-term	Longest due to facilities changes
Associated costs	None	$1,404,420[a]	$1,404,420[a]	$1,404,420[a]	*Option 5.A: 50/50 Split without Changing Rooms:* $29,494 per bay/ $707,856 per building Total: $4,247,136 (Six buildings) *Option 5.B: 50/50 Split with Changing Rooms:* $69,376 per bay/ $1,667,856 per building Total: $10,007,136 (Six buildings) *Option 5.C: 75/25 Split with Changing Rooms:* $95,091 per bay/ $2,282,184 per building Total: $13,693,104 (Six buildings)

	Option One: Integrate Select Training Activities	Option Two: Integrate Flights 50/50 After Fall Out From Sleeping Bays	Option Three: Integrate Flights 50/50 in Sleeping Bays After Morning Hygiene	Option Four: Integrate as Many Flights as Possible with 25 Percent Women (75/25 Option)	Option Five: Integrate Sleeping Bays
Main Takeaways	• Increases GIT the least but has shortest timeline • Least disruptive and lowest cost option	• Fewer flights and trainees could be integrated than Option Four • Would require MTI team model, IT and scheduling changes • Maintains training and mentoring in sleeping bays	• Fewer flights and trainees could be integrated than Option Four • Would require MTI team model, IT and scheduling changes • Would be major departure from current housing and training arrangements	• Allows for more flights and trainees to be integrated than Options One, Two, and Three • GIT can be substantially increased fairly quickly and with modest costs • Maintains training and mentoring in sleeping bays	• Biggest departure from current housing and training arrangements • Most expensive option and longest timeline due to facilities changes

ᵃ These costs include first-year personnel costs for the new MTI team model. This cost includes the addition of an assistant director of operations and the loss of one flight commander per squadron. If the loss of one flight commander per squadron is not offset by the addition of one assistant director of operations, the costs are $558,270. Required IT costs for these options are assumed to be captured in current contracts or already planned and programmed.

The following main conclusions arose from our analysis.

- The optimal option for GIT will depend on USAF priorities.
- The 50/50 and 75/25 options cannot achieve their targeted levels of integration 100 percent of the time.
- The 75/25 option offers the greatest degree of integration on the shortest timeline.
- None of the options are likely to produce critically few women (five or fewer) in training flights.
- The 737th TRG's proposed MTI team model will facilitate GIT and increase leadership opportunities for MTIs.

Recommendations for Planning and Implementation

The planning phase presents the USAF with a critical window of opportunity to develop integration strategies, plans, and policies and put the necessary data systems in place to monitor GIT over time. Insights from the literatures on organizational change and the integration experiences of foreign militaries inform the following recommendations.

- Clarify and communicate the purpose of change.
- Build support for the change.
- Ensure top leadership support and commitment.

- Develop a detailed implementation plan and assign accountability.
- Institute both internal and external oversight of implementation.
- Monitor GIT over time.
- Ensure lasting change.

Acknowledgments

The authors would like to extend thanks to our U.S. Air Force (USAF) sponsors who provided valuable feedback on various briefings over the course of this study. In particular, we would like to thank Maj Gen Mark Brown, Maj Gen Robert Labrutta, Lt Gen Darryl Roberson, Maj Gen Leonard Patrick, Brig Gen Trent Edwards, and Col William Fischer. We are also grateful to the staff at the 737th Training Group at Lackland Air Force Base. In particular, we would like to thank Laura Munro, Donald Steele, Von Whelchel, Robert Wilson, and MSgt Ian Perry for their assistance with our data collection efforts. Keith Carraghan was also very helpful in providing oversight of this research effort.

We also note that we could not have completed this work without the support of subject-matter experts from the USAF, U.S. Army, U.S. Coast Guard, U.S. Marine Corps, and U.S. Navy. We are grateful for their assistance with our efforts to collect data related to their gender-integrated training policies and procedures.

Finally, we also benefited from the contributions of our RAND colleagues. Ray Conley, Kirsten Keller, Bernard Rostker, Laura Miller, Jennifer Kavanagh, and David Orletsky provided incredibly helpful formal peer reviews of this report.

We retain full responsibility for the objectivity, accuracy, and analytic integrity of the work presented here.

Abbreviations

AFB	Air Force Base
BEAST	Basic Expeditionary Airman Skills Training
BMT	Basic Military Training
BTMS	Basic Training Management System
DoD	Department of Defense
DOTMLPF-P	Doctrine, Organization, Training, Material, Leadership and Education, Personnel, Facilities, and Policy
FY	fiscal year
GIT	gender-integrated training
IT	information technology
MTI	military training instructor
OTS	Officer Training School
PAF	Project AIR FORCE
PT	physical training
RDC	recruit division commander
ROTC	Reserve Officer Training Corps
SAPR	Sexual Assault Prevention and Response
SARC	Sexual Assault Response Coordinator
TTMS	Technical Training Management System
TRG	training group
USAF	United States Air Force
USAFA	United States Air Force Academy
USCG	United States Coast Guard
USMC	United States Marine Corps

1. Introduction

Background and Study Purpose

The U.S. Air Force (USAF) has a long history of integrating women; it was the first service to integrate women during and after initial entry training. In January 1949, the USAF was the first service to send qualified enlisted women through the Officer Candidate School at Lackland Air Force Base (AFB). In 1969, the USAF was also the first service to begin a test program to admit women into its Reserve Officers' Training Corps (ROTC) program at select college campuses. It was not until 1976 that the USAF began integrating basic military training (BMT) at Lackland AFB. After this integration, survey results indicated that the USAF was relatively more satisfied with gender integration than other services. In a study conducted by the Blair Commission (a Congressional commission), the USAF was the least likely to support gender-segregated training (U.S. Congressional Commission on Military Training and Gender-Related Issues, 1999).

USAF BMT trainees are currently assigned to all-male and all-female training flights when they arrive at basic training. These flights are the core instructional unit in BMT. A flight sleeps together in the bays and trains together during the day. Many training activities are "same place and same time," meaning that male and female flights carry out the same training activities at the same place and time. However, trainees often cannot interact across flights during these activities. For instance, during classroom training, male and female flights sit in gender-segregated groups. The same is true in the dining hall—male and female trainees sit and eat in their gender-segregated flights. This was also the case for graduation parade until a recent change—now trainees graduate in gender-integrated "heritage flights." Other BMT activities are also gender-integrated, including some physical training (PT) activities and the capstone BMT event—the Basic Expeditionary Airman Skills Training (the BEAST).

Recently, USAF leadership has become concerned that current levels of BMT GIT may not best prepare trainees to "train as they will fight" in the gender-integrated USAF and do not accurately represent to new trainees or the public that diversity is a USAF priority.[1] The USAF asked the RAND Corporation to conduct an assessment of ways to increase gender-integrated training (GIT) in BMT.

Study Approach

This study consisted of five tasks.

---

[1] In most of the operational USAF, men and women live in separate facilities but work in integrated environments.

1. Review the historical rationale for the degree of GIT in BMT and the associated training outcomes.
2. Compare USAF BMT with that of its sister services.
3. Develop a range of options to incrementally and fully gender integrate USAF BMT.
4. Provide a comparative analysis of selected alternatives for gender-integrated BMT, including a cost analysis of the alternatives.
5. Develop an implementation monitoring framework and document findings and recommendations.

Task One consisted of a broad review of the literature on GIT. We began by examining the historical context, rationale, and methods used for GIT in USAF BMT. We then identified the impacts that GIT has on core BMT goals, including readiness, cohesion, and the achievement of training outcomes. In addition, we identified lessons from the experiences of foreign militaries with GIT. Last, we conducted an in-depth analysis of the literature on the potential impacts of "critical mass" to successful gender integration of groups. Critical mass is the concept that without a minimum proportional threshold of women in a group, outcomes for women will suffer.

In Task Two, we compared the current design of USAF BMT with that of its sister services—the U.S. Army, U.S. Coast Guard (USCG), U.S. Navy, and U.S. Marine Corps (USMC). We also compared USAF BMT with other USAF training programs—the U.S. Air Force Academy (USAFA), Officer Training School (OTS), and ROTC. We identified the rationale for GIT in the other services and USAF programs, as well as GIT-related lessons learned.[2] For this task, we carried out site visits to the following six locations.

1. U.S. Army Training Center, Ft. Jackson, South Carolina
2. USCG Training Center Cape May, New Jersey
3. USMC Recruit Depot, Parris Island, South Carolina
4. U.S. Naval Station Great Lakes, Chicago, Illinois
5. USAFA, Colorado Springs, Colorado
6. USAF OTS and ROTC, Maxwell AFB, Montgomery, Alabama.

During these visits, we conducted discussions with subject-matter experts and observed training activities to better understand how the other services and other USAF training programs conduct training and GIT. For our discussions with subject-matter experts, we used a discussion guide to ensure that we covered the range of topics in all of our discussions across the site visits. This discussion guide asked questions related to the current structure of basic training, issues the USAF should consider if it changes the level of GIT in BMT, questions related to the cost of implementing GIT, and questions related to the types of data used to monitor GIT.[3] When we completed our site visits, we compiled our data into a taxonomy, which then allowed us to

---

[2] We did not examine arrangements at USAF technical training because the sponsor asked us to prioritize settings where new personnel have their very first USAF experiences.

[3] This discussion guide can be found in Appendix A.

identify differences across the various GIT models used by other services and other USAF training programs.

The information we collected in Task Two then fed into Task Three, in which we identified a range of options for increasing GIT in BMT. This spectrum of options spans from incremental changes to full integration of all aspects of BMT. This range of options was informed by the GIT models identified during our visits to the other services. As part of this task, we also identified changes that would need to be made in BMT with each option, as well as how these changes would impact issues such as curriculum, time allocation, master schedule, training administration/documentation (database), staff support functions, and trainee housing.

In Task Four, we carried out a comprehensive assessment of the range of options. We assessed each option against a range of criteria, including:

- the degree to which they reflect working and housing conditions in the operational USAF
- the degree of integration across flights and trainees
- the impact on BMT training
- the impact on military training instructor (MTI) model of instruction
- the impact on BMT scheduling
- the impact on BMT facilities
- the impact on BMT information technology (IT) systems
- the timeline for implementation
- the associated costs.

For each option, we identified costs (e.g., changes to current IT systems, personnel increases, and facility modifications). As part of this assessment, we used historical BMT data to assess the feasibility of the GIT options and explore the impact that each option would have on the level of gender integration for BMT training flights and individual trainees. Finally, we used historical BMT data to examine how attrition would impact each of the GIT options as well as BMT training flights with different male/female proportions (in case the USAF decides to integrate all training flights).

Last, in Task Five, we documented the findings from the various analyses conducted during the course of the study and all of the previous tasks to develop a monitoring framework. This framework offers suggestions for how the USAF might monitor the implementation of any changes made to GIT.[4] We also surveyed the literatures on GIT, organizational change management, and the experiences of foreign militaries to identify specific strategies that may facilitate the successful implementation of GIT. Finally, we looked across all of our findings to develop recommendations to the USAF on how to manage and monitor the implementation of any changes to GIT in BMT.

We also note that this study initially set out to identify the specific impact that the degree of GIT has on the achievement of training outcomes. However, we were unable to do so because

---

[4] This monitoring framework can be found in Appendix C.

none of the services implemented GIT under controlled, experimental conditions in which the specific effects of GIT could be isolated from other factors. In addition, there is a dearth of research on the impacts of varying levels of GIT on training outcomes under controlled, experimental conditions.

Organization of This Report

Chapter Two presents findings from the research literature on GIT. The chapter examines the historical context of GIT in the USAF and findings regarding the effects of GIT on readiness and cohesion. Chapter Three discusses the current state of USAF BMT and presents the various models of GIT used by the U.S. Army, USCG, USMC, Navy, and the USAFA, USAF OTS, and USAF ROTC. It also identifies GIT-related lessons learned from the other services. Chapter Four provides a detailed description of the five options identified by the RAND research team for increasing GIT in BMT, as well as an assessment of each of those options and their estimated costs. Chapter Five presents the findings from an analysis in which the RAND research team applied historical BMT data to current facilities constraints and various GIT options. Chapter Six discusses findings from the literature on critical mass, presents findings from our analysis of the effects of historical rates of attrition on various GIT options, and discusses how the findings from that analysis inform questions related to critical mass in BMT training flights. Chapter Seven discusses considerations when implementing changes in GIT at BMT, particularly ways to manage organizational change and implementation lessons learned from foreign militaries. Chapter Eight discusses our approach to developing a framework for implementing changes to GIT in BMT. Chapter Nine presents our conclusions and recommendations. Appendix A presents the discussion guide used during our site visits. Appendix B presents the detailed analysis of our costing methodology and the options for integrating the sleeping bays. Appendix C presents a framework for monitoring the implementation of changes to GIT in BMT. Appendix D presents the RAND Flight Optimization Tool that RAND developed to help BMT staff assign incoming trainees to sleeping bays and training flights and to calculate female attrition in those training flights.

2. Review of Research Literature on GIT Effects

This chapter reviews the current state of the empirical literature regarding GIT—the historical context of GIT and key findings from the literature on GIT, including GIT's effect on readiness and cohesion. It is important to note that relatively little research has compared GIT directly to gender-segregated training under controlled, experimental settings. Therefore, our understanding of the direct causal effects of GIT on specific types of training activities is limited.

The Historical Context of GIT

Women have been present on the battlefield throughout U.S. history, beginning in the Revolutionary War, but initially they had very limited official roles as volunteers, nurses, and caretakers. During World War II, 350,000 women—an unprecedented number—participated in the war effort, and they began to take on new auxiliary roles so that more men could fight in combat (Holm, 1982; Pub. L. 77-554, 1942). However, large numbers of women did not begin to join the military until the 1970s.

From the Advent of the All-Volunteer Force to Operation Desert Storm: 1971–1991

With the introduction of the all-volunteer force and the end of the draft in 1973, there was an increased perception that women were needed to fill the ranks of the volunteer force, and the services were directed to develop contingency plans to increase the participation of women (Devilbiss, 1990, p. 13).[1] In 1976, women were allowed to enter the service academies, and the USAF was the first service to begin GIT at basic training. The Army began mixed-gender training in 1993, and the Navy began mixed-gender training in 1994.

Of the more than half a million U.S. troops deployed to the Persian Gulf during Operations Desert Shield and Desert Storm, approximately 7 percent (about 41,000) were women (U.S. General Accounting Office, 1993, p. 10). This precipitated major changes in policy with regard to the role of women in the military, including a reexamination of exclusionary laws. For instance, in April 1993, President Bill Clinton ordered the services to open combat aviation to women and to investigate other opportunities for women to serve. Later that year, Congress repealed 10 U.S.C. 6015 (the combat ship exclusion), opening most Navy combatant ships to women (except submarines). As a result of these and other policy changes, the number of positions open to women increased substantially.

---

[1] For a comprehensive account of the evolution of the all-volunteer force, see Rostker, 2006.

Gender integration across the services—and gender integration of basic military training specifically—attracted a great deal of attention and scrutiny from Congress, academia, and the media in the late 1990s. The most influential of those policy studies was the Federal Advisory Committee on Gender-Integrated Training and Related Issues and the report of its findings, more commonly known as the Kassebaum Baker Report. In 1997, Secretary of Defense William Cohen established the Kassebaum-Baker committee—a diverse, bipartisan Pentagon panel—to study the current training programs of the military services. The Kassebaum-Baker Panel was the first to carefully examine and assess gender policies in recruit training, particularly in the wake of an incident at Aberdeen Proving Grounds in 1996 involving trainer misconduct.[2]

The panel examined initial entry training programs for the Army, Navy, and USAF and spoke with instructors and recruits. Generally, the panel concluded that GIT employed by the Army, Navy, and USAF resulted in "less discipline, less unit cohesion, and more distraction from the training programs," and therefore recommended all basic training at the platoon, flight, and division-level be conducted in a nonintegrated fashion (Federal Advisory Committee on Gender-Integrated Training and Related Issues, 1997). Furthermore, the panel made specific recommendations on how gender integration should be dismantled, including suggestions that all of the services return to separate gender-segregated barracks for both basic *and* advanced training facilities (Federal Advisory Committee on Gender-Integrated Training and Related Issues, 1997). Members also rejected unrealistic policies for integrated training and living arrangements, such as "no-talk, no touch" rules (Federal Advisory Committee on Gender-Integrated Training and Related Issues, 1997). Cohen rejected the panel's recommendation that the Army, USN, and USAF segregate men and women for much of basic training ("Cohen Rejects Segregating Trainees By Sex At Camp," 1998).

Following the Kassebaum-Baker Panel's recommendations, the USAF responded by explaining points on which it agreed and disagreed. Gen. Michael E. Ryan, the USAF's top officer, told Congress that "such gender separation would be 'counterproductive' to the 'train-as-we-operate' philosophy" (Bowman, 1998). Vice Chief of Staff Paul E. Eberhart also emphasized, "we view the challenge of instilling discipline as a leadership issues, not an organizational issue" (Eberhart, 1998). The USAF's response also noted its focus on meeting the intent of the report's recommendations through a service-unique approach to accomplishing mission readiness, specifically stating that "men and women must work together to accomplish the mission and this begins at BMT" (U.S. Department of the Air Force, 1999). This sentiment appeared to be shared across the services.

---

[2] In November 1996, misconduct by instructors against female trainees at Aberdeen Proving Ground was uncovered. The Army eventually brought charges against 12 commissioned and noncommissioned male officers for sexually assaulting female trainees under their command. See Shadley, 2013.

Shortly before the release of the Kassebaum-Baker panel report, Congress mandated the formation of another panel, tasked with further studying the training of male and female servicemembers in GIT. The Congressional Commission on Military Training and Gender-Related Issues, more commonly known as the Blair Commission, was primarily tasked with reviewing the basic training programs across the services as they related to gender integration. In focus groups conducted by the Blair Commission, leaders did not mention gender when discussing the major issues, challenges, and concerns unless specifically asked and therefore did not consider these problematic or challenging (U.S. Congressional Commission on Military Training and Gender-Related Issues, 1999).

The Blair Commission's recommendations differed from those of the Kassebaum-Baker Committee (U.S. Congressional Commission on Military Training and Gender-Related Issues, 1999). The Blair Commission noted that regardless of the challenges associated with GIT, each service should be allowed to conduct basic training in accordance with its current policies, goals, and training design, because in general, the services' current training was already sustaining mission readiness and the commission found no fundamental differences in readiness or cohesion attributable to gender-training format (U.S. Congressional Commission on Military Training and Gender-Related Issues, 1999).

The Post-9/11 Era

The wars in Iraq and Afghanistan proved to be a watershed in the story of the integration of women into the military. In February 2010, Secretary of Defense Robert Gates notified Congress of the Department of the Navy's desire to reverse the policy of prohibiting women from submarine service. In 2012, the Army announced that it would open as many as 14,000 combat-related jobs in six Military Occupational Specialties at the battalion level. BG Barry Price, the director of human resources policy at the Army G-1 (Personnel), said, "The last 11 years of warfare have really revealed to us there are no front lines. There are no rear echelons. Everybody was vulnerable to the influence of the enemy" (Wong, 2012). In November 2016, Secretary of Defense Ashton Carter announced that all positions in the U.S. military would be opened to women. It is within this historical context of the gradual expansion of women's roles in the military that GIT has also evolved over time.

Key Findings from Literature

It is important to note that the literature indicates that isolating the effects of GIT on military training can be challenging. For instance, many studies examine differences between male and female outcomes individually, rather than differences in outcomes specifically attributable to GIT versus nonintegrated training. Therefore, gender differences in outcomes in these studies do not necessarily reflect successes or failures of GIT, nor do differences in outcomes illustrate best practices for implementing GIT.[3] In addition, much of the literature is from the 1990s, and we do not know if those findings are still relevant today. Despite these challenges, we can draw some general conclusions from the literature. Generally, research suggests that GIT improves female performance and does not adversely affect male performance in terms of both readiness and cohesion (Scarpate and O'Neill, 1992; Simutis and Mottern, 1996; U.S. General Accounting Office, 1996). We examine the effect of GIT on readiness and cohesion in more detail below.

GIT Effects on Readiness

In terms of entry-level training outcomes, readiness may include discipline, knowledge of rules and regulations, acceptance of organizational values, attrition, PT (pre- and post-test physical fitness scores), and technical training (e.g., course content). Generally, the Blair Commission found that the training design and standards for basic training tasks did not fundamentally differ by gender, excluding gender- and age-norming physical fitness testing (U.S. Congressional Commission on Military Training and Gender-Related Issues, 1999). In terms of jobs recently opened to women during that timeframe, the overwhelming majority of women and the majority of men said that the impact of women on unit readiness was not evident or it was positive (U.S. General Accounting Office, 1999). A Navy study also found no impact on objective performance measures for women trained in gender-integrated units compared to gender-segregated units (Scarpate and O'Neill, 1992). Also, Simutis and Mottern (1996) found in a U.S. Army sample that higher physical fitness, marksmanship, and individual proficiency test scores in GIT units compared to gender-segregated units, suggesting that GIT may actually improve women's training performance.

Indeed, physical fitness test scores administered before basic training routinely show that both male and female recruits begin in poor physical condition, and both improve over the course of basic training (Mottern et al., 1997). While some have expressed concern that GIT could harm men's training performance, it is important to note that neither the Army nor the Navy study found that the performance of men was degraded by GIT (Simutis and Mottern, 1996; Scarpate and O'Neill, 1992). In fact, in some cases, GIT improves men's training performance as well. For instance, the U.S. General Accounting Office found that physical fitness and basic rifle marksmanship pass rates for men in gender-integrated companies exceeded that of segregated all-male companies (U.S. General Accounting Office, 1996).

Some also make the argument that GIT allows trainees to "train as they will fight" when they are assigned to an operational unit. While few studies have been able to isolate the impacts of specific levels of GIT on training outcomes, some qualitative data have assessed trainees' perceptions of the impacts of GIT. For instance, in one study, more than two-thirds of

---

[3] The literature on gender-segregated civilian education has also had difficulty isolating the effects of gender-segregated education on outcomes, and there is no consensus on whether gender-segregated schools are more effective in enhancing educational outcomes than coeducational schools (American Association of University Women Educational Foundation, 1998; Datnow and Hubbard, 2002; Mael et al., 2005; Park et al., 2013).

8

respondents from the Army, Navy, and USAF (and just over one-third of the USMC) stated that having men and women in basic training made it easier to adapt once in integrated operational units (Dooley, 1998). Even among USMC recruits who stated that gender-segregated basic training was most effective, some noted that eventually men and women would need to integrate before they could perform together in operational settings (Dooley, 1998). U.S. military officials have also reported that increased roles for women in the military and society have positively affected the training environment (U.S. General Accounting Office, 1996). In the current debate surrounding levels of gender integration in BMT, others have argued that BMT is not the operational USAF and that trainees should be segregated during BMT so that they can focus on transforming into airmen with as few distractions as possible.

It is also important to note that there remains a great deal of uncertainty regarding whether gender-segregated training or GIT yields higher performance outcomes. For instance, in 2014–2015, the USMC conducted a large experiment that examined the impacts of integrated, gender-neutral training in the execution of both individual and collective training tasks within ground combat arms occupational specialties. The experiment found that all-male units outperformed integrated units on most measures, including the time to complete tasks, move under load, and achieve timely effects on target (U.S. Marine Corps Operational Test and Evaluation Activity, 2015). Integrated units performed at lower overall levels, completed tasks more slowly, and fired weapons with less accuracy than all-male units (U.S. Marine Corps Operational Test and Evaluation Activity, 2015). Female marines also sustained significantly higher injury rates and demonstrated lower levels of physical performance capacity overall (U.S. Marine Corps Operational Test and Evaluation Activity, 2015). The methodology of this study has come under attack by some, including the secretary of the Navy and some members of Congress. There was some concern that the women who volunteered to participate in the experiment may not have been representative of the types of women that are interested in USMC infantry positions and who are able to pass the physical fitness standards to join the USMC infantry (Myers, 2016).

Effect of GIT on Cohesion

Cohesion refers to the psychological forces acting on individuals to remain as members of a group. In general, prior research demonstrates that more cohesive groups perform better than less cohesive groups (Beal et al., 2003; Castaño et al., 2013; Evans and Dion, 2012). Several studies have found significant relationships between cohesion and various measures of individual and group performance (Oliver et al., 1999; Mullen and Copper, 1994; Beal et al., 2003). Importantly, there is also evidence that the link between cohesion and performance is bidirectional (Mathieu et al., 2015). Mullen and Copper's (1994) analysis revealed that unit cohesion increases performance, but that increasing unit performance leads to greater unit cohesion. In fact, the evidence suggests that the effect of performance on cohesion is stronger than the effect of cohesion on performance (Mullen and Copper, 1994). Thus, increasing cohesion can increase performance, but performing well can also increase cohesion.

Cohesion is often cited as a primary outcome of basic training. Furthermore, cohesion is highlighted as a criterion of interest for GIT. Some previous research has been conducted on the impact of GIT and cohesion. For instance, where comparisons were possible, the Blair Commission found there were no effects of training format (gender-integrated versus nonintegrated) in terms of morale, enthusiasm, commitment, cohesion, or motivation of recruits in basic training that were directly attributable to the gender format of the training (U.S. Congressional Commission on Military Training and Gender-Related Issues, 1999; Johnson, 1999). Through focus groups conducted across the services, the Blair Commission also found that officers and experienced enlisted servicemembers reported that gender only became an issue in units that were already experiencing conflict (Laurence et al., 1999).

Some research also indicates that GIT improves teamwork measures for both men and women compared to nonintegrated training (Scarpate and O'Neill, 1992). Other research indicates that GIT may foster, rather than harm, cohesion. For instance, GIT reduces stereotypic perceptions regarding female recruits and increases favorable perceptions of women's motivation and character (Boldry et al., 2001). Conversely, gender-segregated training can perpetuate feelings of superiority among men, which results in arrogance toward women (Halpern et al., 2011). The Blair Commission also found that individuals across the services who had worked with the opposite gender to a greater extent had more positive attitudes about GIT (Ramsberger et al., 1999, p. 46). In addition, female marines completing boot camp prior to the integration of Marine Combat Training in October 1996 reported feeling less accepted as members of the USMC team compared to those who completed boot camp after this change (Dooley, 1998).

However, concerns regarding the possibility that GIT may negatively affect cohesion are not without merit. For instance, group members are more likely to interact more with members within their own subgroups. This decreases communication with other subgroups, and may therefore reduce cohesion for the group as a whole (Dreachslin, Hunt, and Sprainer, 2000; Hogg and Terry, 2000). Accordingly, the research literature shows that more homogeneous groups exhibit greater group cohesion (O'Reilly, Caldwell, and Barnett, 1989) and fewer relational conflicts (Jehn, Northcraft, and Neale, 1999; Pelled, Eisenhardt, and Xin, 1999).

Based on site visits and focus groups from all the services' training facilities, and after conducting discussion groups with over 1,000 trainees, 500 instructors, 375 first-term servicemembers, and interviewing over 275 supervisors at operational units, the Kassebaum-Baker panel concluded that integrated units split by separate housing requirements cannot achieve cohesion at a level comparable of same-gender training units (Report of the Federal Advisory Committee on Gender-Integrated Training and Related Issues, 1997). Although it is difficult to draw conclusions across services, USMC trainees (who are not gender-integrated during training) scored the highest on attitudes considered conducive to cohesion. In fact, female marine trainees scored highest among all graduates on these attitudes (Johnson, 1999, p. 155; Report of the Federal Advisory Commission on Gender-Integrated Training and Related Issues to the Secretary of Defense, 1997, p. 16). Furthermore, GIT can highlight differences between physical fitness standards, may create resentment among men and therefore undermine the training unit's cohesion, or can even be used to justify discrimination against female recruits (Stiehm, 1989; Snyder, 1999).

Mitigation Strategies to Foster Readiness and Cohesion

While the effect of GIT on basic training outcomes (including readiness and cohesion) is mostly neutral or positive, additional strategies can be taken to mitigate any potential negative effect of GIT. Below, we identify two mitigation strategies, based on our review of the literature.

Minimize Injuries When Implementing GIT

A number of studies note that women exhibit higher injury rates and in some cases underreport health problems during training (Boldry et al., 2001; DeFleur et al., 1985). Presumably, this is due to high motivation to pass training (Boldry et al., 2001). This can create a particularly challenging situation for both trainees and trainers, as female trainees who hide or ignore medical problems or injuries are also blamed for being overmotivated and irresponsible in these situations (Boldry et al., 2001; Bijur et al., 1997). However, higher female injury rates are not necessarily attributable to GIT. Indeed, higher injury rates and underreporting health concerns also occurred when units were gender-segregated (Sasson-Levy and Amram-Katz, 2007). Clearly, injuries negatively affect training success, and therefore readiness. Reducing injuries offers a direct path to reduce attrition, and many interventions seeking to reduce injuries are not gender specific and therefore aid both men and women.

Reducing injuries during BMT requires both physical and cultural solutions. Developments in PT, including improvements in training equipment and facilities, advances in sports medicine, and the use of athletic shoes for PT, have all aided PT and help both women and men reduce injuries (U.S. General Accounting Office, 1996). In many cases, equipment, rather than gender per se, is the primary cause of injuries. Equipment and uniforms are often designed for men and may not meet the needs of women. Ill-fitting clothing, equipment, and training materiel can cause injury and result in training and assessment limitations. A number of potential solutions exist, such as providing appropriate or adjustable equipment or allowing personnel to buy or select their own equipment and uniforms. In most cases, these cost differences are negligible (U.S. General Accounting Office, 1996). Many of these modifications also benefit men by having equipment and uniforms that are appropriate across body types—both male and female.

Finally, there appears to be a cultural component to injuries. Previous research has shown that female trainees may hide or ignore injuries,[4] but this behavior is likely due to the context, rather than gender per se. For instance, in a qualitative study of Israeli Defense Force soldiers completing basic training in both integrated and nonintegrated bases, women in the integrated base underreported injuries. Women in the nonintegrated base, however, did not underreport, and

---

[4] See Bijur et al., 1997, pp. 456–61; DeFleur et al., 1985.

accordingly, showed injury rates much higher than their integrated peers. At first glance, this appears to support gender-segregated training to facilitate the reporting of injuries and seeking medical attention when needed. Upon closer investigation though, it was revealed that a rumor spread in the integrated base claiming that trainees exempted for medical reasons for more than five days would be dismissed from the course, effectively deterring both male and female trainees from reporting injury rates. Thus, it appears that when injuries are accepted as part of training, underreporting health concerns ceases to be a problem (Sasson-Levy and Amram-Katz, 2007). Transparent policies regarding injuries sustained over the course of BMT and the importance of seeking medical attention when necessary are likely to reduce underreporting of injuries, regardless of gender. Although rumors cannot always be identified in time to be remedied, they may be preempted with clear explanations for why seeking medical attention is valued and what the consequences are for ignoring or hiding injuries.

Role Modeling

Role models act as exemplars of culture, which can influence the norms and expectations regarding proper relationships between the sexes, particularly for new members of that culture. MTIs are role models of USAF culture. Indeed, leading by example is a basic tenet of command and sets the tone across a training unit. Instructor attitudes towards GIT can and do affect recruits' readiness and cohesion. For example, during previous waves of integration, Army drill sergeants who expressed negative views about GIT trained poorer soldiers with lower morale (Mottern et al., 1997). Also, during this time, USMC recruits expressed concern that USMC leaders needed additional training and education to understand and exemplify the GIT phase of basic military training to improve acceptance of women in the USMC and military readiness (Dooley, 1998). It is also important to note that sensitivity to the military instructors' workload is also likely important for success. Previous research has found that trainers dissatisfied with the training environment can be due to changes such as increasing workload, rather than dissatisfaction with GIT itself (Ramsburger et al., 1999, p. 466; Laurence et al., 1999, pp. 286, 301–302, 308).

Deliberate attempts at providing role modeling in terms of GIT appear effective. Additionally, it may be advantageous for cohesion and role modeling for recruits to see mixed-gender leadership working and relating to one another in a positive way (Dooley, 1998). It does not appear that role models must be matched by gender, as long as same-gender role models are visible. For example, women in male-dominated fields show greater performance when they can observe successful female role models—even if they are not their direct reports (Marx and Roman, 2002). In practical terms, when trainees only interact with MTIs of their same gender, this distorts the reality of gender-integrated leadership throughout the USAF and arguably does not prepare trainees for future assignments in which their commanders may be of the opposite gender.

Conclusions from the Literature

As evidenced by our review in this chapter, it is important to note that relatively little research has examined GIT directly in comparison to gender-segregated training under controlled, experimental settings. Therefore, our understanding of the direct causal effects of GIT on specific types of training activities is limited. Generally though, research suggests that GIT improves female performance and does not adversely affect male performance in terms of both readiness and cohesion. For instance, a Navy study found no impact on objective performance measures for women trained in gender-integrated units compared to gender-segregated units (Scarpate and O'Neill, 1992). Also, Simutis and Mottern (1996) found higher physical fitness, marksmanship, and individual proficiency test scores in a sample of GIT Army units compared to a sample of gender-segregated units, suggesting that GIT may actually improve women's training performance. While few studies have been able to isolate the impacts of specific levels of GIT on training outcomes, some studies have assessed trainees' perceptions of the impacts of GIT. For instance, in one study, more than two-thirds of respondents from the Army, Navy, and USAF (and just over one-third of the USMC) stated that having men and women in basic training made it easier to adapt once in integrated operational units (Dooley, 1998).

While the effect of GIT on basic training outcomes (including readiness and cohesion) is mostly neutral or positive, additional strategies to mitigate any potential negative effect of GIT can be taken. Minimizing injuries and role modeling are two such important strategies to mitigate potential negative effects of GIT. The next chapter discusses our findings regarding the other services' models for GIT.

3. Service GIT Models

As mentioned in Chapter One, we visited the following six locations:

1. U.S. Army Training Center, Ft. Jackson, South Carolina
2. USCG Training Center Cape May, New Jersey
3. USMC Recruit Depot, Parris Island, South Carolina
4. Naval Station Great Lakes, Chicago, Illinois
5. USAFA, Colorado Springs, Colorado
6. USAF OTS and ROTC, Maxwell AFB, Montgomery, Alabama.

During these visits, we conducted discussions with subject-matter experts and observed training activities to better understand how the other services and other USAF training programs conduct basic training and GIT. For our discussions with subject-matter experts, we used a discussion guide to ensure that we covered the range of topics in all of our discussions across the site visits. This discussion guide asked questions related to the current structure of basic training, issues the USAF should consider if it changes the level of GIT in BMT, questions related to the cost of implementing GIT, and questions related to the types of data used to monitor GIT.[1]

This chapter summarizes the data collected during these site visits.[2] The chapter provides summaries of the models of GIT used by all of the services and other USAF training programs. These summaries focus on: (1) facilities, (2) training and instruction, (3) safeguard policies, and (4) the rationale for GIT in that service or training program. We begin this chapter by reviewing the current state of USAF BMT and then discuss the models of GIT used by other services and other USAF training programs.

Current State of USAF BMT

Currently, USAF trainees are assigned to male and female flights as they arrive to BMT at Lackland AFB. Two flights are paired together so that they can conduct the same types of training activities concurrently. Female flights ("sister flights") are always paired with male flights ("brother flights"); due to the lower numbers of female flights, many male flights are paired with other male flights. Despite this pairing, much of BMT training is what we term "same place and same time"—male and female flights carry out the same training activities at the same place and same time, but trainees do not interact across flights. Some examples of these "same place and same time" activities include classroom training, some PT, some inspections, training in the sleeping bays, and "instructor time" (when MTIs meet with their flights to discuss

---

[1] This discussion guide can be found in Appendix A.

[2] During our site visits, the individuals we spoke with could provide information on current beliefs and experiences with GIT, but could not speak about institutional history and past challenges as facilities, policies and practices have been changed.

different topics). During other activities, such as the BMT capstone exercise—the Basic Expeditionary Airman Skills Training (the BEAST)—men and women work together in integrated teams. Until 2015, the BMT Airmen's Run, Coin Ceremony, and graduation parade were also conducted in separate male and female flights. With the introduction of gender-integrated "Heritage Flights," male and female airmen now reorganize during their last week of training from gender-segregated squadron training flights into gender-integrated flights composed of other male and female trainees in their career fields. When trainees graduate BMT, their follow-on technical training in their career fields is gender-integrated.

Facilities

In considering various options for increasing GIT, it is also important to note that four new BMT dormitory buildings have recently been built, and two more will be completed over the next few years. Therefore, any modifications to facilities would need to be made to these new buildings. The sleeping bays are located on the second, third, and fourth floors of each of these buildings. Each of those floors has eight sleeping bays (two on each of the four sides of the building), for a total of 24 bays per building. Men and women are housed in the same dormitory building, but use separate sleeping bays. The entry doorways to the sleeping bays are locked, and a multiple-step security process is required to gain access to the sleeping bays.

Figure 3.1 presents the current floorplan of the sleeping bay area. Each bay is U-shaped, with 26 beds and lockers on each side of the "U," for a total of 52 beds. A three-fourths–high wall separates the two sides of the bay, which allows MTIs to give direction to trainees on both sides of the bay at once. There is a latrine with toilets, sinks, and showers. There is also an office space for MTIs, a dayroom, and a laundry room with a closet for storing trainees' luggage.

Figure 3.1. Current Sleeping Bay Layout

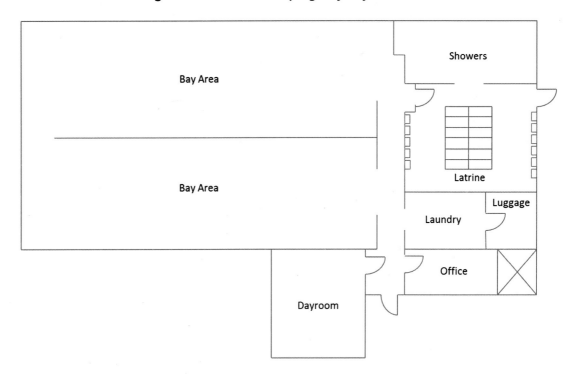

SOURCE: U.S. Air Force Air Education and Training Command, undated.

Each bay is identical. The beds are the same, the wall lockers are the same, and the blankets and pillows are all arranged the same. In fact, the beds and lockers are so much alike that each one is numbered to help trainees quickly find their bed and locker. The only differences in the sleeping bay areas are the location of the latrine and dayrooms, which differ slightly due to building design. Even the latrines are the same, so that they can accommodate either all-male or all-female flights.

Training and Instruction

As described above, USAF BMT trainees are currently assigned to all-male and all-female training flights. These flights are the core BMT instructional unit. A flight sleeps together in the bays and trains together during the day. As indicated above, many training activities that these male and female flights conduct are "same place and same time." For instance, during classroom training, male and female flights sit on either half of the classroom as gender-segregated groups. The same is true when male and female flights enter the dining hall—male and female trainees sit and eat in their gender-segregated flights. Until a recent change, the graduation parade was also segregated by gender; now trainees graduate in gender-integrated "heritage flights." Other activities are gender-integrated, including the BEAST.

The current BMT model of instruction includes a lead MTI and a support MTI (known as the "tap out") for each flight. While these two MTIs are intended to lead a flight as a team, our discussions with MTIs and BMT administrators indicate that this is not always the case and that the lead MTI often maintains control over the flight. MTIs can be assigned to both male and female flights, but female flights must have at least one female MTI.

Safeguard Policies

In considering various options for increasing GIT in BMT, it is critical to understand that in 2012, 17 MTIs were accused of sexual misconduct with female trainees.[3] This incident, as well as broader attention to sexual harassment and sexual assault in the military, have prioritized the creation of a safe training environment and the protection of trainees from abuse. As a result, the USAF has made many modifications to the training environment (including facilities) and established an oversight council that monitors progress on an ongoing basis. Many safeguard policies were also put into place to protect against harassment and assault of trainees by trainers. For instance, MTIs are no longer allowed to sleep in the trainee sleeping bays or in the dormitory buildings. In addition, there are windows in MTI offices, so that any activity in the offices can be easily observed, and MTIs are prohibited from being alone with a recruit behind closed doors. MTIs are also prohibited from entering an opposite-gender squad bay without another MTI. Especially in the wake of this incident, the safety of trainees will be paramount when making any changes to GIT.

In addition, policies are also in place to prevent and respond to sexual harassment and sexual assault by trainees against other trainees. Such policies include the installation of dorm hotlines that allow trainees direct telephone access to chaplains and Sexual Assault Response Coordinators (SARCs) without having to involve MTIs. In addition, the USAF has a "wingman" policy, in which trainees are assigned a wingman, who serves as a partner during basic training so that trainees are never alone.

GIT Rationale

The rationale for the current model of GIT in BMT has largely been driven by the facilities— in particular, the size and configuration of the sleeping bays. Since male and female trainees sleep in gender-segregated flights, this has determined the level of GIT in those same training flights. Having the same flight sleep together and train together certainly makes the logistical and scheduling aspects of BMT easier, but USAF leaders have begun to consider whether a different model of GIT could offer additional training benefits. USAF leaders have raised concerns that the current model does not accurately represent to new trainees or to the public that diversity is a USAF priority, and that current levels of GIT do not reflect integrated working conditions in the operational USAF—especially now that all USAF positions are open to women. There is also

---

[3] On June 20, 2012, an independent, commander-directed investigation by Brig Gen Margaret Woodward revealed sexual misconduct by military training instructors against female trainees at Lackland AFB between October 2010 and June 2011. See U.S. House of Representatives Committee on Armed Services, 2013.

concern that gender-segregated training flights in BMT could potentially hamper recruitment efforts.

GIT Models Used in Other Services and USAF Training Programs

We next turn to our analysis of enlisted basic training across the other services and the GIT models used by the other services. Table 3.1 summarizes the findings from this analysis.

Table 3.1. Summary of Enlisted Basic Training Across the Services and in USAF Officer Training

	Facilities	Training	GIT Rationale
Air Force (enlisted)	• Open bays • Men and women sleep separately	• Male and female recruits train in separate flights • Some training activities are gender-integrated • Some training activities are gender segregated	Facilities have largely driven the configuration of male and female flights
Army (enlisted)	• Open bays • Men and women sleep separately • "Separate and secure" system of safeguards	• All training platoons fall out and intermix in the morning • All aspects of training are gender-integrated	• Trainees have to be prepared to work in gender-integrated operational assignments • Bays are viewed as only places to sleep and shower, rather than training areas
Coast Guard (enlisted)	• Open bays • Bays are somewhat integrated	All training activities are gender-integrated	Recruits have to be prepared to work in gender-integrated operational environments
Marine Corps (enlisted)	Female trainees are housed in a separate barracks area that has its own dining facility and PT course	Male and female recruits initially train separately, but same place and same time training increases over time	Segregated training minimizes distractions and allows trainees to see role models and mentors of the same gender
Navy (enlisted)	• Open bays • Men and women sleep separately • Half of the men and women switch bays	• All aspects of training are gender-integrated • GIT also takes place in the bays	Recruits have to prepared to work in gender-integrated operational assignments
USAFA/OTS/ROTC (officer)	• College dorm-style facilities that are integrated	• All aspects of training are gender-integrated	• Women were in separate dorm buildings for only six months after USAFA integrated • Trainees treated as adults at OTS/ROTC • Trainees have to be prepared to work in gender-integrated operational assignments

Table 3.2 provides a summary of the safeguard policies used by the other services and other USAF training programs to prevent harassment and assault of trainees by both trainers and other trainees.

Table 3.2. Summary of Safeguard Policies Used by Other Services and Other USAF Training Programs

General Safety	Instructor Safety
No tolerance policy for fraternization, assault, and harassment	Instructors not allowed to sleep in bays
Locked doors on sleeping bays	Instructors not allowed to enter the bays at night
Cameras that monitor bays and dorms	Large windows on instructor offices
Trainees must sleep in PT clothing	Instructors not allowed to meet with trainees alone behind closed doors
Require battle buddy/wingman system for trainees	Male and female instructors paired together so they never enter a sleeping bay alone
Sexual Assault Prevention and Response (SAPR) phones are easily accessible	Instructors cannot contact students via email or Facebook during training or after they graduate

Army

The RAND team visited the U.S. Army Training Center at Fort Jackson, South Carolina. We were told that in fiscal year (FY) 2015, approximately 44,000 enlisted Army trainees went through basic training at Fort Jackson. For about the first week after arriving at Fort Jackson, new recruits live close to the in-processing center and are placed in temporary groups during in-processing activities, such as medical appointments, clothing issue, and haircuts. Recruits do not move to their assigned training group or dormitory until in-processing is complete.

The core unit for Army basic training is a company of 240 soldiers—typically 180 men and 60 women.[4] This company typically has three platoons of 80 soldiers (60 men and 20 women). Each company has 12 drill sergeants. At least one of those drill sergeants must be female, but the Army has a target of three female drill sergeants per company. These female drill sergeants take ownership of training for female-specific issues, such as women's hairstyles and feminine hygiene.

Facilities

Like the USAF, male and female trainees at Fort Jackson are housed in gender-segregated sleeping bays. When trainees fall out in the morning, two male sleeping bays integrate with one female sleeping bay to form an integrated company of three platoons. This integrated company is about one-third women and two-thirds men. As a result, Army trainees are members of both a gender-segregated sleeping bay and a GIT company. In the Army model, the sleeping bays are

---

[4] When there are higher numbers of women in an incoming class, this number can fluctuate up to 120 men and 120 women.

viewed as strictly a place to sleep and take care of personal hygiene. The only types of training activities that are conducted in the sleeping bays are inspections of the bays and personal lockers.

In response to the Aberdeen incident described in Chapter Two, the Army instituted an elaborate system of safeguards called "separate and secure." This system requires multiple security steps to gain access to the sleeping bays, and a series of cameras monitor the building hallways and bays. Instructors are prohibited from entering the sleeping bays at night between 10 p.m. and six a.m.

During our visit, we heard concerns that while the separate and secure system was developed to protect trainees from harassment and assault by instructors, it may provide a safe haven for recruits to harass each other while instructors are not present. Some drill sergeants indicated that because they are prohibited from going into the sleeping bays at night, they are hesitant to take care of issues that arise at night in the bays for fear of punishment.

Training and Instruction

As described above, in the morning, male and female sleeping bays fall out and intermix to form an integrated company of three platoons. One set of drill sergeants oversees each sleeping bay, while other drill sergeants oversee the training platoons. The RAND team asked if trainees get confused about having multiple sets of drill sergeants or if trainees play instructors against one another; we were told that this is not a problem.

Once the platoons are integrated, all training activities are gender-integrated. This includes classroom instruction, combat skill development, and the capstone field event. The Army Physical Fitness Test standards are different for men and women, but PT is fully gender-integrated. For instance, runs are conducted by ability group regardless of gender, and integrated squads, not individuals, conduct the obstacle course. To prevent injuries, both men and women are prevented from carrying more than 30 percent of their body weight. Marksmanship and hand grenade training are also integrated. The PT uniforms for both men and women include an integrated spandex liner for additional discretion. When in the sleeping bays, trainees need to be clothed in at least their PT uniforms.

The Department of the Army currently selects basic training drill sergeants—85 to 90 percent of drill sergeant assignments are nonvoluntary. Drill sergeants must complete a training course, and the Army now requires them to have a security clearance.

Safeguard Policies

The Army's safeguard policies focus on preventing and responding to sexual harassment and sexual assault perpetrated by both trainers and trainees. For instance, the Army has a "Battle Buddy" policy, in which trainees are assigned a same-gender battle buddy, who basically serves as a partner during basic training so that trainees are never alone. There are also Sexual Harassment/Assault Response and Prevention phones in the sleeping bays that trainees can use to report incidences of sexual harassment or sexual assault. However, to preserve anonymity, these phones can also be used for many other purposes, including checking the weather. At the company level, company victim advocates—noncommissioned officers who undergo victim advocate training—are available to assist trainees. At the brigade level, SARCs are an additional resource for trainees.

GIT Rationale

The Army's current rationale for GIT is that it better prepares trainees for their future assignments in the integrated operational Army. It also prepares men and women to work together in a professional environment and reinforces to trainees that both men and women have gone through the same training. Having a gender-integrated instructor corps reinforces to trainees that Army leadership is integrated.

Coast Guard

RAND visited USCG Training Center Cape May to observe how the USCG conducts its enlisted recruit basic training program. Of all of the services, the USCG conducts the most gender-integrated enlisted basic training program—all training activities are gender-integrated, as are the sleeping bays to some extent. The USCG basic training program is 53 days long, and recruits train in integrated groups called "companies."

The USCG is different from the other services in important ways. The USCG is the smallest of the services. During our site visit, we were told that in FY 2015, 3,500 recruits entered USCG enlisted basic training (3,250 active duty and 150 reserve). Another important difference is that unlike the other services, which have additional training (e.g., technical training or advanced training) that follows basic training, 95 percent of USCG recruits who complete basic training are then assigned directly to an operational unit in the USCG fleet. Therefore, USCG basic training is meant to mimic life in such an operational unit.

Facilities

Like the USAF and Army, Cape May has open-bay sleeping facilities called "squad bays." These squad bays are the most gender-integrated sleeping facilities among all the services. The squad bays are large rooms that have rows of beds. These beds have "coffin lockers" under each of them, which allow recruits to store their uniforms and other personal items. The squad bays are arranged to reflect the layout of maritime vessels in the operational USCG.

The squad bays are divided into two spaces. Women sleep at one end of the bay and have their own latrine, with showers, toilets, sinks, and a changing area. A partial wall and door separates the male and female areas of the bay. Women must transit the male section of the bay to get to the entrance of the bay. Before transiting through the male part of the squad bay, women must stand at the threshold to the male space, face the wall, slap the wall three times, and yell "female requesting transit." The men must then yell "secure the head," and they must make sure the entrance to their latrine is fully closed with a curtain. Once the men yell "head secured," women can then walk through the male space of the bay, but as they walk across the space, they must yell "female transiting, female transiting, female transiting." When the women have finished crossing the male space, they must yell "female transit complete." All recruits must be fully clothed in physical fitness uniforms when in the sleeping bay. It is important to note that both male and female latrines have areas where recruits can change into their clothes. Men are allowed in female squad bays for official business. This includes security rounds at night, but there are always two recruits paired up when on watch.

Training and Instruction

USCG recruits train in gender-integrated companies, and all training activities are gender-integrated. The USCG uses the Cooper Fitness Institute's guidelines for physical fitness for men and women. The USCG has found that the best predictor for whether or not a recruit will graduate basic training is whether or not he or she can complete the mile-and-a-half run. Attrition is 26 percent for those who cannot complete the run, but for those who can complete the run, attrition is only 6 percent.

USCG basic training instructors are called "company commanders." The selection process for company commanders is very competitive and heavily scrutinized. During a recent search for instructors before our visit, of the 55 applicants, 12 were women and 43 were men. Like the other services we visited, the USCG expressed to us that recruiting female instructors can be a challenge because there are fewer women in the USCG, and even fewer of those may be interested in instructor positions. The USCG has a detailed manual of standard operating procedures that outlines policies, procedures and expectations for the behavior of training instructors.

Safeguard Policies

Like many of the other services, the USCG implemented policy changes after instances of inappropriate behavior between instructors and recruits, largely due to a lack of supervision over the instructors. For instance, instructors and recruits initiated relationships with one another during basic training, and some instructors began dating recruits after they graduated. As a result, the USCG established new rules that prohibit instructors from having a relationship with recruits until a year after the recruit has graduated. In addition, the USCG prohibits instructors from staying in the recruit dormitory buildings after 10:30 p.m. Recruits are also not allowed into instructors' offices, and there are cameras on every floor of the dormitory buildings. In addition, there is a two-person integrity rule—instructors cannot be alone with a recruit behind closed doors. At night, teams of recruits are designated as "fire watches"—sentries who patrol the sleeping bays to ensure that things are in order.

The USCG also has policies in place to prevent and respond to sexual harassment and sexual assault. For instance, within the first 24 hours of basic training, recruits are given a sexual assault briefing. Two weeks into basic training, they are given a two-hour briefing by the SARC.

GIT Rationale

The USCG's unique mission set, small force, and operational structure provide the rationale for its high level of GIT. Given that USCG recruits move from basic training directly to an operational unit, the USCG believes that they need to prepare their recruits to work in a gender-integrated environment—one that often includes confined quarters on a small boat.

Marine Corps

The USMC enlisted basic training program is the most gender-segregated of all the services. Most activities in USMC boot camp are gender-segregated, but as training progresses, some training events are "same place and same time" but not fully integrated. The Marine Corps believes the gender-segregated recruit training model enables young men and women to focus on transforming from civilians to marines without distractions, and to develop a strong initial foundation for marine standards and their identity as a marine. The Marine Corps believes this model also provides a balance of strong same-gender and mixed-gender role models for recruits to emulate, while simultaneously enabling same place and same time training. The RAND team visited USMC Recruit Depot Parris Island—the only location where enlisted female marine recruits go through boot camp, as well as male marine recruits from the eastern half of the country. Male recruits typically arrive at Parris Island 44 weeks out of the year. Women arrive at Parris Island 24 weeks out of the year—a fairly consistent intake of 130 women every other week. Currently, women are approximately 7 percent of the USMC (Perkins, 2015).

Facilities

A single Recruit Training Regiment is divided into four training battalions (three male and one female), all with their own separate barracks areas with open squad bays, physical trainers, and their own PT courses. Two of the male battalions primarily utilize a consolidated dining facility, with the other using a dining facility within its barracks area. Female recruits are housed in their own barracks area, which has its own dining facility, PT course, and physical trainers. However, female recruits utilize many of the depot's common facilities at the same time as male recruits. These include the Recruit Training Facility academic building; the Water Survival Combat training pool; the Martial Arts and Confidence Course area; the rifle ranges; the rappelling and fast rope training facilities; chemical, biological, radiological, and nuclear training facilities; the depot's main parade deck, where recruits perform their initial and final drill evaluations and the graduation parade; the All-Weather Training Facility; and the Marine Corps Community Services facilities, chapel, and Religious Ministries Center.

Training and Instruction

USMC recruit training was consolidated under a single Recruit Training Regiment in 1986, and since then, all recruits (regardless of gender) are required to complete the same 70 training days, follow the same training program of instruction, and complete the same graduation requirements. Follow-on Marine Corps entry-level training at the School of Infantry has been gender-integrated since 1997.

Most training activities during USMC boot camp are gender-segregated, although as training progresses, some activities are conducted at the same place and same time. For instance, both male and female platoons may be on the confidence course at the same time, but they will be on different parts of the course and do not interact. This is also the case with the Crucible (the capstone event of the USMC enlisted basic training program). Male and female platoons are on the Crucible course at the same time, but they never tackle the same event on the course at the same time. During graduation, male and female platoons are on the parade field at the same time, but they march in their separate platoons. Individual recruits do not interact with members of other platoons (regardless of gender) during the parade under any circumstance. It should be noted that the commander of troops alternates between male and female company commanders, and the parade staff is integrated.

Like the Army, the platoon is the key training unit in USMC boot camp, and platoons are led by drill instructors. Training platoons have same-gender drill instructors, but other instructors may be of the opposite gender (e.g., classroom, rifle-range, water survival, and martial arts program instructors). There are at least three drill instructors assigned to each platoon. The senior drill instructor is the team leader; the other drill instructors are responsible for teaching knowledge, close order drill, and making corrections. Most of the drill instructors we spoke with could not imagine moving toward a team-based instructor model like other services. In addition, since drill instructors are rated on all aspects of their platoon's performance, competition among the platoons is fierce. This competition is a source of great pride among the platoons and the drill instructors, and the USMC feels strongly that this competition elevates everyone's performance.

Lastly, the drill instructors we spoke with also emphasized that the time spent in the squad bays mentoring and training is key to the "transformation" process in which a civilian is transformed into a marine—"it is where the magic happens."

The drill instructors felt strongly that any attempts to increase GIT would jeopardize that transformation process. However, there have been a number of increases in gender integration in the last 12 months.

- Some physical fitness events have become same place and same time, including recruit final physical fitness test and final combat fitness test events.
- Rappel tower and gas chamber training have become same place and same time.
- Marksmanship training is integrated where and when possible, with male and female recruits on the same firing lines.
- Several staff assignment changes have been made that facilitate mixed-gender leadership in traditionally single-gender training battalions. Female executive officers have been assigned to male training battalions, and male executive officers have been assigned to female training battalions; female first sergeants have been assigned to male training battalions and male first sergeants assigned to female training battalions; and female commanders have been assigned to male training battalions.

Safeguard Policies

The USMC has a "Battle Buddy" policy in which recruits must never be alone without their same-gender battle buddy. In addition, as stated in Marine Corps Order 1510.32F, "supervision is the key to proper execution and the safe conduct of recruit training" (U.S. Department of the Navy, 2012).

GIT Rationale

The USMC rationale for gender-segregated training during boot camps has several different elements. First, the USMC argues that gender-segregated training minimizes distractions and allows recruits to focus on their training. Second, the USMC argues that gender-segregated boot camp allows trainees to see strong role models and mentors of the same gender. There are so few women in the USMC that female recruits may not see female role models or mentors for much of their careers. Third, the USMC argues that the current system produces high-quality female marines and that altering the current recruit training construct may jeopardize some of the "intangibles" of the transformation process that transforms civilians into marines. The current system of team-building at the platoon level seeks to raise expectations for individual performance, instill high levels of confidence, and maximize physical fitness while minimizing injuries. All training that follows boot camp is gender-integrated, the drill instructor school is integrated, and female leaders are spread across the leadership structure at Parris Island.

Navy

The RAND team also visited Naval Station Great Lakes, Illinois, the Navy's only location for enlisted recruit training. In FY 2015, 40,283 enlisted Navy recruits went through basic training at Naval Station Great Lakes (Recruit Command, February 2016), a number comparable to the number of enlisted trainees at USAF BMT. The first four to 11 days after new recruits arrive to Naval Station Great Lakes are called "processing days." During this time, recruits take care of all of their in-processing activities, including paperwork, medical appointments, clothing issue, and haircuts. This processing time allows the Navy to fill training groups to their optimal size. Sometimes, a training group fills completely and there are only a few recruits remaining from the arrival group; they are held as the first recruits for the next training group. In other cases, a training group does not quite fill up, and recruits must wait until the next group of recruits arrives to begin training. Recruits do not move to their assigned training dormitory until processing days are over.

Facilities

Like all the services except for the USCG, Navy recruits sleep in segregated all-male and all-female open sleeping bays. The Navy calls these sleeping bays "compartments" or "houses." Each sleeping bay normally houses 88 recruits. The walls in the sleeping bays are moveable to accommodate fluctuating training group sizes. Male and female sleeping bays are located across the hallway from one another and they are laid out identically to one another—even the beds are numbered the same. The doors from the sleeping bays to the hallway are usually open, and there are no locks on the doors to the bays.

Inside each sleeping bay, there is a latrine with showers, sinks, toilets, and a changing area. The entrance to the latrine is designed so that trainees need to walk around a wall to get to the sinks, showers, toilets and changing area—the wall blocks any sight lines from the main area of the sleeping bay into the latrine. In the main area of the sleeping bay, recruits have to wear at least their PT clothes. The design of the latrines and the clothing policy allow instructors of the opposite gender to be in the sleeping bay without broaching recruit privacy. Opposite gender instructors cannot be in the sleeping bays before morning reveille and after evening "lights out."

In the morning, after reveille and morning hygiene, an instructor yells "integrate," and half of the men and women switch sleeping bays and form two integrated training groups called "divisions." For accounting purposes, the recruits that switch bays stand next to the bed that is numbered the same as the one they are assigned to in their original sleeping bay. Once the divisions are integrated (50-percent men/50-percent women), they then fall out and train as integrated divisions all day until evening hygiene, when they return to their gender-segregated sleeping bays. All of the dormitory buildings have their own dining facilities, so integrated divisions also dine together.

Like the Army model, the USN model creates an interesting dynamic, in which recruits are both members of their gender-segregated sleeping bay and their GIT division. It is important to note that since there are not enough women to integrate all training divisions at such a high proportion, many of the training divisions remain all-male.

Training and Instruction

In integrated brother/sister divisions, almost all aspects of recruit training are gender-integrated. This includes classroom training, PT, fire safety, and the capstone exercise. In addition, GIT also takes place in the sleeping bays. When divisions are integrated in the sleeping bays for training during the day, they undergo activities such as mentoring, classroom instruction, and uniform inspections. Recruits do not touch each other's personal items on beds or in lockers. The only activities that are gender-segregated require training or inspection of things that cannot be moved (e.g., the sleeping bay, beds, personal lockers). Those inspections are carried out as a gender-segregated house rather than by integrated division.

Since Navy recruits shift between gender-segregated sleeping bays and GIT divisions like the Army model, this model requires a team approach to instruction. In the Navy model, there are six instructors, called "recruit division commanders" (RDCs), per two divisions. This gender-integrated team of six RDCs oversees two sleeping bays that form two integrated training divisions. This model requires RDCs to communicate very well with one another. This teamwork is reinforced by the fact that RDCs are not given awards for individual performance but are only acknowledged if the entire RDC team does well. The Navy has found that this model has cut down on misconduct that can stem from an overly competitive environment among instructors.

One potential concern with such a team model is that there will be inconsistencies across instructors and training divisions. To ensure that standards are taught consistently across divisions, quality assurance inspectors conduct routine inspections on various training standards and then compare the results across divisions. These inspectors are RDCs who are on a scheduled break from their usual duties. (This break usually happens in the middle of the RDC assignment and allows RDCs to recharge and work on other duties, such as quality assurance inspections or overseeing recruits during processing days.)

Safeguard Policies

The Navy has instituted several policies to safeguard against misconduct among recruits and instructors. For instance, fraternization among recruits is immediately addressed when discovered and fraternizers are often held accountable publicly during "open" Captain's Mast as an example to other recruits.[5] In addition, within the division, recruits are designated as "rovers" at night to monitor their sleeping bays. These rovers are the same gender as the recruits in the inspected bays. Policies are also in place to prevent misconduct among instructors. For instance, a "no isolation policy" prohibits RDCs from being alone with a recruit behind closed doors. If the RDC needs to meet with a recruit, the door must be open or another recruit or instructor must be in the room. In addition, RDC offices have large, glass windows so that recruits can see into the offices. Feedback on the RDCs is collected after all three major tests during recruit training, and there is a midcycle review with a fleet commander (the RDC's department head) in which further feedback about RDCs is solicited. Lastly, recruits can drop cards in boxes outside the chaplains' office, requesting to make appointments to discuss any of their concerns.

GIT Rationale

The Navy integrated training in 1994. Like the USCG, the Navy's rationale for GIT is that recruits need to be prepared to work in a gender-integrated environment when they go into the operational fleet. For instance, sailors on ships and submarines walk back and forth from berthing areas to latrines in their bathrobes. The Navy also believes that if recruits see instructors of different genders, it reinforces the message to recruits that the leadership structure of the Navy is also gender-integrated and that their future commanders may be members of the opposite gender.

---

[5] Captain's Mast is the procedure used by the Navy to impose nonjudicial punishment.

USAFA, USAF OTS, and USAF ROTC

We also visited the USAFA in Colorado Springs, Colorado, and USAF OTS and USAF ROTC at Maxwell AFB in Montgomery, Alabama, to better understand how they conduct USAF officer training. The findings from our site visits are summarized below.

Facilities

The USAFA, OTS, and ROTC all have college dorm-style facilities. Men and women live in the same dorm buildings. Individual rooms have same-gender occupants, but occupants in the rooms next door or across the hall could be of the opposite gender. Men and women walk down the hall from their dorm rooms to use the male and female latrines—often in bathrobes or pajamas.

Training and Instruction

All aspects of training at the USAFA, OTS, and ROTC are gender-integrated, including classroom instruction and PT. The combatives course is a good example of how GIT varies across USAF training programs. For instance, at the USAFA, the combatives course is fully integrated. Men and women are put into integrated classes, and they fight each other based on their weight—not their gender. At ROTC, the combatives class is integrated, but matches are not—men are only allowed to fight men and women are only allowed to fight women. The USAFA is also considering fully integrating the boxing class so that men and women will box each other.

The instructor cadre is also gender-integrated across the USAFA, OTS, and ROTC, and instructors teach both men and women.

Safeguard Policies

The USAFA, ROTC, and OTS have policies in place to safeguard against sexual assault and sexual harassment. For instance, at the USAFA, students cannot be behind closed doors with a member of the opposite gender. Students also are not allowed to sit on a horizontal surface (e.g., a couch, bed, or desk) with a member of the opposite gender. At OTS, dormitory rooms have individual locks, and there are security cameras in the dormitory hallways. OTS trainees receive a SAPR briefing within 24 hours upon arrival, and SAPR phones are available in the dormitories. At OTS, instructors are no longer allowed to use Facebook to contact students. OTS instructors are also not allowed to enter a student's room alone.

GIT Rationale

The rationale for GIT at the USAFA, OTS, and ROTC is that trainees need to be prepared for assignments and deployments in the operational USAF. During our visits, we were told that the method of gender-integrated instruction and the dorm-style housing arrangements help prepare men and women to work and live together.

Advice from Other Services and USAF Training Programs

The other services and the other USAF training programs offered the following advice to the USAF as it decides whether and how to increase GIT in BMT.

- Mimic what right looks like.
- Don't make it too hard.
- Don't let women feel differently.
- Rethink fraternization and harassment—include male-on-male and female-on-female fraternization and harassment.
- Create a culture of teamwork and communication.
- Fire those people that will not support change.
- Keep in mind that recruits do not know the difference between what they are going through and previous policies.
- Society is integrated; do not create an artificial environment in BMT.
- By not integrating basic training, trainees can focus on transforming into airmen with fewer distractions, and female trainees can develop strong bonds with female instructors.

4. Options for Increasing GIT and Their Associated Costs

Fully integrating BMT would require assigning incoming female trainees across all training flights. To do this, BMT staff would need to know ahead of time how many female trainees will arrive at BMT each week or assign female trainees to training flights after all trainees have arrived at BMT and the total number of women in the incoming class can be determined. Since the number of BMT slots is driven by the number of USAF technical training seats available and it is difficult to know how many women will actually arrive at BMT during any particular week, assigning trainees to flights ahead of time will likely continue to be unfeasible. To assign female trainees to flights after all trainees have arrived, significant changes would need to be made to the way that trainees are currently in-processed. In the meantime, other options exist to substantially increase GIT in BMT on a shorter timeline and with fewer major changes and costs. This chapter focuses on five such options.

After visiting USAF BMT, similar training in other services, and USAF officer training programs, RAND identified five options for increasing GIT in BMT.

1. Integrate select training activities.
2. Integrate flights 50-percent male/50-percent female after they fall out from sleeping bays.
3. Integrate flights 50-percent male/50-percent female in the sleeping bays after morning hygiene.
4. Integrate as many flights as possible with 25 percent women (75/25 Option).
5. Integrate sleeping bays.

The development of these options was informed by our literature review and the service models discussed in the previous chapter, as well as consultations with our sponsor regarding USAF priorities. In this chapter, we identify two overarching issues that could facilitate GIT in BMT, discuss in detail the set of options for increasing GIT in USAF BMT, and provide our assessment of each option.

Overarching Issues That Could Facilitate GIT in BMT

During our visits to the other services, we identified two concepts that could facilitate GIT in BMT: (1) the concept of a "processing flight," and (2) a MTI team concept of instruction. Both of these issues could be incorporated into the options discussed in this chapter. We discuss both the concept of processing flights and a MTI team concept in more detail below.

Consider Establishing "Processing Flights"

In our site visits to the services, we discovered that most services consolidate all in-processing activities (e.g., clothing issue, medical exams, haircuts) into the first few days after arrival and assign trainees to a temporary "processing flight" for in-processing. However, the USAF assigns trainees to training flights the evening that they arrive at basic training. Then, over the next few days (called "Zero Week"), MTIs conduct training instruction alongside in-processing activities. The same MTI responsible for successfully getting a new trainee to graduation also carries the burden of navigating that trainee through all of the in-processing appointments during Zero Week.

At the request of our sponsor, the RAND team examined the pros and cons of establishing "processing flights." We outline the benefits and challenges associated with the concept of a processing flight in more detail below.

Processing Flights Could Foster Integration

Many MTIs reported to the RAND team that during Zero Week, they are torn between administrative requirements, in-processing appointments, and training. For instance, often trainees must go back to medical for a follow-up or back to individual equipment issue for the proper piece of clothing or equipment. In addition, in-processing requirements are not the same for men and women (e.g., women have additional medical tests). Some MTIs we spoke with expressed concern that if BMT implements GIT flights, the competing demands of Zero Week will only be exacerbated because they will have to keep track of both men and women in their training flights during Zero Week. Some MTIs we spoke with said that GIT would be facilitated if all in-processing activities were consolidated into the first few days and military training began only when in-processing was complete. That way, both trainees and MTIs could focus on training.

Processing Flights Could Provide an Opportunity for MTIs to Recharge

Most MTIs graduate a flight on Friday, ship those graduates to Airmen's Week very early Monday morning, and pick up a new group of trainees on Tuesday night. MTIs' hours are long, and their mission requires constant attention. Processing flights would give the MTIs a short break and the opportunity for a different routine. If Zero Week was entirely dedicated to in-processing, an MTI would graduate a class on Friday and ship them to Airmen's Week very early Monday morning, then have a week until picking up a new group on the Tuesday of the next week. During this week, MTIs could recharge their batteries.

Today, some MTIs "push" flights for two years before they move to another job within BMT for a rest from the relentless pace of graduation, picking up a new flight, graduation, picking up a new flight, etc. By assigning MTIs to processing flights, the MTI would get a periodic short-term break from pushing flights, and the new trainees would continue to learn those important first lessons from an MTI. This benefits both the MTIs and the USAF as a whole.

An Opportunity to Assign Trainees to Training Flights More Systematically

Another benefit to processing flights relates to how training flights are formed. When new USAF trainees arrive at Lackland AFB for BMT, flight assignment is primarily driven by arrival time. If trainees are first assigned to temporary processing flights as they arrive, BMT officials could change this method. Processing flights could also enable gender integration by providing BMT officials the time to identify the total number of women that have arrived at BMT each week; officials could then proportionally assign those women across all BMT flights.

Logistics Are a Main Challenge

Logistics are one of the main challenges with establishing processing flights. The ability to house new trainees during Zero Week in facilities separate from other trainees is important. One option may be to use older dorm facilities at Lackland AFB; however, fully investigating feasibility will require an in-depth analysis.

In-Processing Contractors Will Need to Be Consulted

Another potential concern with the concept of processing flights is whether the contractors that provide in-processing services could accommodate a shorter in-processing schedule. This would need to be confirmed before further developing the processing flight concept.

A New MTI Team Model

Implementing several of the GIT options below will likely require that BMT adopt a new team model for MTIs. Given that trainees will be shifting between sleeping bays and training flights, MTIs will need to coordinate more with each other and develop a team-based approach to instructing trainees. The 737th TRG has proposed such a MTI team model. RAND analyzed this proposed MTI model and does not have any further suggestions to refine it. We describe the current and proposed model in more detail below.

Currently, BMT squadrons are very flat organizations. The current model is depicted in Figure 4.1. One squadron commander and one operations officer supervise four flight commanders. Each of these four flight commanders is in charge of a section. These flight commanders each supervise one instructor supervisor who then oversees six flights. Each flight of trainees has two MTIs assigned, for a total of 12 MTIs. With four sections per squadron, there are 48 line MTIs in the squadron and only four leadership positions (instructor supervisors) available. This flat organization leaves little room for leadership positions for MTIs. For current MTIs to assume leadership roles, outside of becoming an instructor supervisor, they must leave the squadron and work on the basic training staff in a support role. When RAND spoke with MTIs, many expressed frustration about these limited leadership opportunities.

Figure 4.1. Current BMT Flight Configuration and Manpower Requirements

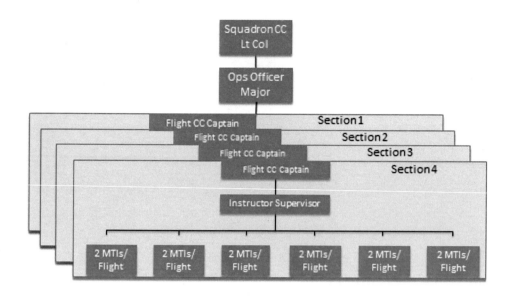

The 737th's proposed MTI team model, as depicted in Figure 4.2, adds two additional instructor supervisor positions to each squadron. This new model also reduces the number of sections per squadron to three instead of four. Each of those three sections has one squadron commander, one operations officer, and one repurposed assistant operations officer. Each of the three sections has a flight commander and two instructor supervisors. Each section has eight training flights, with two MTIs for each training flight.

Figure 4.2. Proposed MTI Model

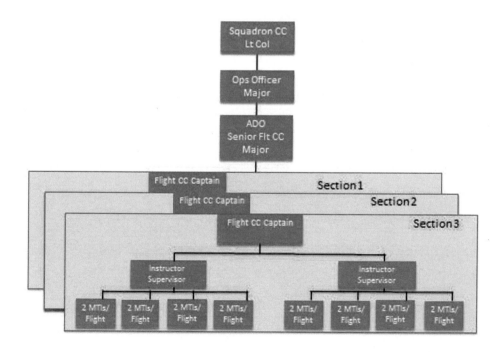

The new MTI team model results in a net addition to personnel. The net difference between the current and proposed MTI models per squadron is an increase of two instructor supervisors for each squadron and the reduction of one flight commander for each squadron.[1] However, the loss of one flight commander per squadron is offset by the addition of one assistant director of operations. These changes would apply to each of the six training squadrons; therefore, the total net difference is an increase of 12 instructor supervisors. The overall effect based on these changes is a modest increase in personnel costs.

Table 4.1 below summarizes the cost of these changes in the first year. The personnel costs were estimated based on an Office of the Undersecretary of Defense memorandum (2015) for FY 2016 Department of Defense (DoD) military personnel composite standard pay rates.[2] The proposed model assumes that half of the instructor supervisors are E-7s and half are E-8s. These paygrades are summarized in the cost per position column in Table 4.1.

Table 4.1. Cost Summary for MTI Team Model with Assistant Director of Operations

Personnel Changes	Number of Positions	First-Year Cost per Position	First-Year Total Cost (FY 2016$)
Increase in Instructor Supervisors	+12	$117,035	$1,404,420
Net Change in Cost			**$1,404,420**

If the loss of one flight commander per squadron is not offset by the addition of one assistant director of operations, the costs are summarized in Table 4.2.

Table 4.2. Cost Summary for MTI Team Model without Assistant Director of Operations

Personnel Changes	Number of Positions	First-Year Cost per Position	First-Year Total Cost (FY 2016$)
Increase in Instructor Supervisors	+12	$117,035	$1,404,420
Decrease in Flight Commanders	–6	$141,025	–$846,150
Net Change in Cost			**$558,270**

Next, we turn to an assessment of the options for increasing GIT in BMT.

---

[1] The current model has four instructor supervisors per squadron, while the proposed model has six instructor supervisors per squadron.

[2] Office of the Under Secretary of Defense, "FY 2016 Department of Defense (DoD) Military Personnel Composite Standard Pay and Reimbursement Rates," Memorandum for Deputy Assistant Secretary of the Air Force (Financial Management and Comptroller), Washington, D.C., March 9, 2015. The annual DoD composite rate includes the following military personnel appropriation costs: average basic pay plus retired pay accrual, Medicare-eligible retiree health care accrual, basic allowance for housing, basic allowance for subsistence, incentive and special pay, permanent change of station expenses, and miscellaneous pay.

Option One: Integrate Select Training Activities

There are opportunities to increase GIT without changing all-male/all-female bays and all-male/all-female flights. For instance, many of the BMT training activities that are categorized as "same place and same time" could be integrated without changing the current structure and composition of training flights and without impacting the current BMT schedule. Classroom instruction, some PT activities, drill, and meals are examples of training events and activities that offer opportunities to increase GIT. With a few changes in policies and procedures, these activities could be integrated (or further integrated in the case of PT).

For instance, currently, brother/sister flights participate in the same joint classroom instruction. However, given the way in which training flights file into the room, the all-male flight sits on one side of the room and the all-female flight sits on the other side of the room. The line down the middle of the room between male and female trainees is invisible but omnipresent. However, instructors could allow or direct trainees to sit randomly in the classroom. This change in policy would increase GIT, introduce trainees to those outside their flight, and expose trainees to people from different backgrounds and different parts of the country.

PT also presents an opportunity where GIT could be increased without significant effort or disruption. Currently, brother/sister flights often conduct PT at the same place and same time, but not all PT activities are gender-integrated. While not all PT activities need to be gender-integrated, there may be opportunities for integrating more PT activities. When men and women participate in the same type of PT challenges together as a team, the bonds of camaraderie and respect begin to take root.

Finally, the dining facility is another place where GIT could be reinforced with no changes to scheduling or other disruptions. As with classroom instruction, all-male flights sit separately from all-female flights in the dining facility. Again, this is largely a function of how the flights file into the dining facility. Allowing male and female trainees to sit together, without regard for gender, will allow them to interact with trainees outside of their training flight.

This option would not make fundamental changes to BMT. Rather, this option would allow the USAF to increase GIT while maintaining the current structure of all-male and all-female training flights and the current BMT schedule. Table 4.3 summarizes our assessment of Option One.

Table 4.3. Option One: Integrate Select Training Activities

Degree to which option reflects working and housing conditions in the operational USAF	• Simulates segregated sleeping conditions in the operational USAF • Only somewhat simulates integrated working conditions in the operational USAF
Degree of integration across flight and trainees	Increases GIT the least
Concerns over critical mass	No concerns over critical mass
Impact on where BMT training occurs	• Maintains the current gender-segregated flight structure • Maintains training and mentoring in sleeping bays
Impact on MTI model of instruction	No change to current MTI model of instruction
Impact on BMT scheduling	Does not require any scheduling or logistical changes
Impact on BMT facilities	No facilities modifications required
Impact on BMT IT systems	Does not require any scheduling or logistical changes
Timeline for implementation	Shortest timeline for implementation
Associated costs	None
Main takeaways	• Increases GIT the least but has shortest timeline • Least disruptive and lowest-cost option

Assessment of Option One

This option is the least disruptive and the lowest cost of all the options, and as a result, it also has the shortest implementation timeline. Under this option, BMT operations at Lackland AFB would continue without significant disruption, as this option does not require major scheduling or logistical changes.

However, this option increases GIT the least and maintains the current gender-segregated flight structure. These minimal changes may not be enough to provide trainees with sufficient integrated interactions to actually have significant benefits. In addition, since this option makes such minor changes, it would be difficult to assess whether changes in outcomes are really a result of changes in GIT.

Potential Costs

Since this option would require no modifications to sleeping bays and no changes to the current IT systems used to assign and track trainees, it has no costs associated with it—making it the least expensive of the five options.

Option Two: Integrate Flights 50/50 After Fall Out from Sleeping Bays

The second GIT option would require a few more changes to current BMT policies and procedures than the first option, but they would have a significant impact on increasing GIT.

Currently, a training flight sleeps in an open bay and in the morning it leaves its bay (or "falls out") for formation on the drill pad and subsequent training activities. In other words, a training flight sleeps in the same space at night and then trains together during the day.

This second GIT option is a hybrid between the Navy model of GIT and the Army model of GIT. This option would retain the current BMT sleeping arrangements in the bays, in which bays are comprised of all-male (brother) or all-female (sister) flights. However, under this second option, after the trainees fall out for training in the morning, half of the men from one bay would combine with half of the women from another bay to form one GIT flight, comprised of half men and half women. After this integrated flight forms in the morning, it would then conduct the day's training activities as an integrated group. When training is complete for the day, this integrated flight would then disband; men and women would return to their respective same-gender sleeping bays. Table 4.4 summarizes our assessment of Option Two.

Table 4.4. Option Two: Integrate Flights 50/50 After They Fall Out from Sleeping Bays

Degree to which option reflects working and housing conditions in the operational USAF	Most closely simulates segregated sleeping and integrated working conditions in the operational USAF
Degree of integration across flight and trainees	• Fewer training flights could be integrated than under Option Four • Integrated flights would have very high levels of integration (50%)
Concerns over critical mass	No concerns over critical mass
Impact on where BMT training occurs	• Training and mentoring activities could be maintained in in sleeping bays or moved to other venues • Members of the same bay would also be members of different training flights; this could potentially cause confusion • Could pose challenges for standardization of training
Impact on MTI model of instruction	• MTI team model could provide trainees with more role models and mentors, and MTIs with more leadership opportunities • MTI team model may require an adjustment period
Impact on BMT scheduling	Could create more complex scheduling issues
Impact on BMT facilities	No facilities modifications required
Impact on BMT IT systems	Requires a change to IT systems used to assign and track trainees
Timeline for implementation	Medium term timeline for implementation
Associated costs	$1,404,420[a]
Main takeaways	• Fewer flights and trainees could be integrated than Option 4 • Would require MTI team model, IT and scheduling changes • Current housing arrangements could be maintained

[a] These costs include first-year personnel costs for the new MTI team model (the addition of an assistant director of operations and the loss of one flight commander per squadron). If the loss of one flight commander per squadron is not offset by the addition of one assistant director of operations, the costs are $558,270. Required IT costs for these options are assumed to be captured in current contracts or already planned and programmed.

Assessment of Option Two

This option would allow more trainees to experience GIT than under the current BMT model, but the limited number of female trainees would mean that not all training flights could be integrated. Some male trainees would continue to train in all-male training flights. There is a tradeoff between integrating a few training flights with high proportions of women and integrating more flights with lower proportions of women. This tradeoff is discussed in detail in Chapter Seven. Because women would be integrated into training flights at high percentages in this option, overall, fewer training flights could be gender-integrated. Therefore, fewer male and female trainees would experience GIT under this option than under Option Four.

This option would also form a unique group dynamic. Each trainee becomes part of two different groups: the group where he or she sleeps and the flight with which he or she trains. This would be a departure from the current model of BMT and would require a different model of instructor oversight—one in which MTIs work as a team to coordinate oversight of both bays and training flights. Since this option requires trainees to shift between sleeping bays and training flights, it could also potentially pose challenges for training standardization across training flights as well as across sleeping bays. However, the other services' team instructor models indicated that standardization of training can be enforced through increased coordination among instructors.

Option Two would also require changes to training policies and procedures on several fronts. First, training activities would no longer be conducted in the sleeping bays and would need to be relocated. Training and mentoring activities that currently take place in the bays (e.g., keeping wall lockers, beds, and the bay to standards; handing out mail; counseling trainees) would need to be moved to other venues, such as the drill pad or classrooms. The MTIs that we spoke with seemed divided on whether mentoring and training time in the bay should be eliminated or moved. Some felt that the time in the bay should be protected from any changes, while others expressed that any changes would require a change in mindset but would be feasible (and had been done in the past). This option would require changes to accountability policies and procedures, since trainees would shift between the sleeping bays and different training flights.

Finally, a MTI team model, such as the one proposed in this option, could provide trainees with more role models and mentors and provide MTIs with more leadership opportunities. However, such a change may require new guidance on how MTIs coordinate with one another and new responsibilities for those who oversee MTIs and instructors. In addition, a MTI team model may also require an adjustment period in the way MTIs coordinate with one another, as well as how they adjust to the new command structure in the proposed MTI team model.

Potential Costs

Broadly speaking, the only foreseeable costs associated with this option are for changes to the IT systems used to manage BMT and for personnel hiring to fit the new MTI team model for

GIT. Currently, the USAF uses the Basic Training Management System (BTMS) to manage BMT personnel. BTMS provides information and automated data processing capabilities to support all aspects of BMT (e.g., recruit training administration, trainee accountability, and flight training scheduling). The system allows key decisionmakers to use current and historical training information to gauge the effectiveness of the BMT program or to support USAF requirements for special programs. A contractor currently manages operations and sustainment for BTMS. The contractor performs all maintenance activities, including any perfective maintenance required as a result of new user requirements due to GIT.[3] Subject-matter experts stated that additional costs might accrue if development needs to greatly accelerate as a result of GIT; otherwise, the marginal changes required would likely be accounted for in the existing contract.

Eventually, BTMS will be absorbed by the Technical Training Management System (TTMS). TTMS is used by Air Education and Training Command and subordinate technical training wings to design, develop, deliver, evaluate, report, and manage training. The merger of the two systems will better integrate BMT with technical training management. This merger has been planned and programmed and any software changes required as a result of GIT will be absorbed by TTMS.

This option would also require a MTI team model to increase coordination across MTIs. The proposed change from the current MTI model to the proposed MTI team model carries a modest increase in personnel costs (see Table 4.1 and Table 4.2).

Option Three: Integrate Flights 50/50 in Sleeping Bays After Morning Hygiene

The third option would require a few more changes to current BMT policies and procedures than the second option but would have even more of an impact on increasing GIT. This option is similar to the Navy model of GIT. Under this option, men and women would still sleep in separate bays, but after morning hygiene, in which they brush their teeth and get dressed, brother and sister flights would integrate in the sleeping bays (unlike Option Two, in which trainees integrate on the drill pad).

Like Option Two, half of the men from one bay would combine with half of the women from another bay to form one GIT flight. In this case, half of the men from the male bay would walk over to the female sleeping bay, and half of the women from the female bay would walk over to the male sleeping bay. After forming in the bays, these flights would conduct the day's training activities as integrated groups. Late in the evening, when training is completed for the day, the men and women would switch back to all-male and all-female sleeping bays for last minute clean-up and sleep. Table 4.5 summarizes our assessment of Option Three.

---

[3] Perfective maintenance includes development required to implement new or changed user requirements meant to enhance the functionality of the software.

Table 4.5. Option Three: Integrate Flights 50/50 in Sleeping Bays After Morning Hygiene

Degree to which option reflects working and housing conditions in the operational USAF	Does not simulate segregated sleeping and integrated working conditions in the operational USAF
Degree of integration across flight and trainees	• Fewer training flights could be gender-integrated than under Option Four • Flights that are integrated would experience very high levels of gender integration (50%)
Concerns over critical mass	No concerns over critical mass
Impact on where BMT training occurs	• Maintains training and mentoring time in sleeping bays • Members of the same bay would also be members of different training flights; this could potentially cause confusion • Could pose challenges for standardization of training
Impact on MTI model of instruction	• MTI team model could provide trainees with more role models and mentors, and MTIs with more leadership opportunities • MTI team model may require an adjustment period
Impact on BMT scheduling	Could create more complex scheduling issues
Impact on BMT facilities	No facilities modifications required
Impact on BMT IT systems	Requires a change to IT systems used to assign and track trainees
Timeline for implementation	Medium term timeline for implementation
Associated costs	$1,404,420[a]
Main takeaways	• Fewer flights and trainees could be integrated than Option 4 • Would require MTI team model, IT, and scheduling changes • Would be major departure from current housing and training arrangements

[a] These costs include first-year personnel costs for the new MTI team model. This cost includes the addition of an assistant director of operations and the loss of one flight commander per squadron. If the loss of one flight commander per squadron is not offset by the addition of one assistant director of operations, the costs are $558,270. Required IT costs for these options are assumed to be captured in current contracts or already planned and programmed.

Assessment of Option Three

This option has the same tradeoff as Option Two in terms of the number of training flights that could be integrated. This option would allow more trainees to experience GIT than under the current BMT model, but not all training flights could be integrated. This option would also require changes to training policies and procedures on several fronts. First, training activities (e.g., keeping their wall lockers, beds and the bay to standards, handing out mail, and counseling) could continue to be conducted in the sleeping bays as they are now. According to seasoned MTIs, a lot of mentoring, coaching, and teaching take place in the open bay area. Under this option, MTIs would still have mentoring time in the bay with their gender-integrated flights. However, some adjustments would need to be made as to whether specific training occurs with members of a GIT flight or members of a gender-segregated sleeping bay. In addition, like Option Two, this option would require changes to accountability policies and procedures, since trainees will be shifting between the sleeping bays and different training flights.

Like Option Two, members of a GIT flight would also be members of two different sleeping bays. This would be a departure from the current model of BMT and, like Option Two, would require a different model of instructor oversight—one in which MTIs work as a team to coordinate oversight of both the bays and the training flights.

Potential Costs

The potential costs of implementing this option would be similar to Option Two, with similar IT system impacts and personnel cost changes. The same BTMS and TTMS impacts would be relevant, and, like Option Two, the costs are assumed to be captured in current contracts or already planned and programmed for. Like Option Two, this option would also require a MTI team model to increase coordination across MTIs. The proposed change from the current MTI model to the proposed MTI team model carries a modest increase in personnel costs (See Table 4.1 and Table 4.2).

Option Four: Integrate As Many Flights as Possible with 25 Percent Women (75/25 Option)

This option was proposed by the 737th TRG as means to increase GIT. Coincidentally, this option is also similar to the Army model of GIT. Option Four is similar to Option Two, as it would retain the current BMT gender-segregated sleeping arrangements in the bays and those bays would then fall out for training in the morning and intermix. However, under Option Four, trainees would form GIT flights that are 25 percent female and 75 percent male.[4] After forming in the morning, these flights would then conduct the day's training activities as integrated groups. When training is complete for the day, this integrated flight would then disband; the men would return to their respective sleeping bays and the women would return to their respective sleeping bays. Table 4.6 summarizes our assessment of Option Four.

---

[4] We did not include a 75/25 option for integrating in the bays because that would be difficult to do logistically.

Table 4.6. Option Four: Integrate As Many Flights as Possible with 25 Percent Women (75/25 Option)

Degree to which option reflects working and housing conditions in the operational USAF	Most closely resembles sleeping and working conditions in the operational USAF
Degree of integration across flight and trainees	Allows for larger proportion of flights and trainees to be integrated
Concerns over critical mass	Potential critical mass concerns if women are less than 15% of a flight
Impact on where BMT training occurs	• Training and mentoring activities could be maintained in in sleeping bays or moved to other venues • Members of the same bay would also be members of different training flights; this could potentially cause confusion • Could pose challenges for standardization of training
Impact on MTI model of instruction	• MTI team model could provide trainees with more role models and mentors, and MTIs with more leadership opportunities • MTI team model may require an adjustment period
Impact on BMT scheduling	Could create more complex scheduling issues
Impact on BMT facilities	No facilities modifications required
Impact on BMT IT systems	Requires a change to IT systems used to assign and track trainees
Timeline for implementation	Medium term timeline for implementation
Associated costs	$1,404,420[a]
Main takeaways	• Allows for more flights and trainees to be integrated than Options One, Two, and Three • GIT can be substantially increased fairly quickly and with modest costs • Current housing arrangements could be maintained

[a] These costs include first-year personnel costs for the new MTI team model. This cost includes the addition of an assistant director of operations and the loss of one flight commander per squadron. If the loss of one flight commander per squadron is not offset by the addition of one assistant director of operations, the costs are $558,270. Required IT costs for these options are assumed to be captured in current contracts or already planned and programmed.

Assessment of Option Four

This option would allow even more trainees to experience GIT than any of the previous options, and this option would enable the most integration in the shortest timeframe. Like Options Two and Three, under this option, each trainee would become part of two different groups: the group where he or she sleeps and the flight with which he or she trains. Therefore, like Options Two and Three, this option would require a team model of MTI instruction, as well as changes to accountability policies and procedures to track trainees as they shift between sleeping bays and different training flights. In addition, standardizing instruction across bays and training flights will be key to ensuring that training standards remain consistent. This option does not require any modifications to the sleeping bays and would maintain current procedures for conducting training and mentoring activities in the sleeping bays.

Potential Costs

The potential costs of this option would also likely be the same as Options Two and Three, with similar IT system impacts and personnel cost changes. The same BTMS and TTMS impacts would be relevant, and like Options Two and Three, the costs are assumed to be captured in current contracts or already planned and programmed for. This option would also require a MTI team model to increase coordination across MTIs. The proposed change from the current MTI model to the proposed MTI team model carries a modest increase in personnel costs (see Table 4.1 and Table 4.2). Therefore, the costs for this option are the same as the costs associated with Options Two and Three.

Option Five: Integrate Sleeping Bays

The fifth option for increasing GIT at USAF BMT represents the most integrated option. With relatively minor modification to sleeping bays, male and female trainees could serve side-by-side in all aspects of basic training, including in sleeping bays. This option is similar to the option that the USCG uses today.

Integrating sleeping bays is the most costly option due to facility impacts. The USAF is currently in the process of building new training facilities at Lackland AFB, including six buildings (one for each squadron), housing the trainees. Unfortunately, any modifications to the facilities as a result of bay integration would likely require waiting until the completion of the construction. With construction completed on two of the facilities and construction beginning on the final two buildings in FY 2019 and FY 2020, it is not feasible to change design plans now and reprogram military construction funding to accommodate those changes. Furthermore, it is preferable to have uniform facilities; therefore, it is undesirable to modify only those facilities that have not begun construction. Given these constraints, the most likely scenario is modification of the facilities upon their completion.

The RAND team identified three options for modifying the bays to allow integration:

1. 50/50 split of the sleeping bay without changing rooms
2. 50/50 split of the sleeping bay with changing rooms
3. 75/25 split of the sleeping bay with changing rooms.[5]

Each of these options includes unique modifications that are discussed in Appendix B. The modifications presented in Appendix B represent potential solutions to modify the sleeping bays to allow for integrated bays. It should be noted that while the modifications are suggestions, there are likely other potential solutions; however, the options chosen are among the most logical and cost effective given the current sleeping bay layout.[6] We do emphasize that any modifications would need to take into account impacts on carefully designed facilities. For

---

[5] We did not include a 75/25 option without a changing room because that would be logistically difficult.

[6] The modifications accounted for minimal remodeling and rework, such as rerouting major plumbing components.

instance, the air handling system in the current bays was designed to minimize the spread of germs and infections—air conditioning pushes air and germs down to the ground and away from trainees. Any modifications to facilities that could disrupt carefully planned HVAC systems would need to be carefully scrutinized.

As discussed in Chapter One, four new BMT training buildings have already been built and two more will be completed over the next few years. The sleeping bays are located on the second, third, and fourth floors of each of these buildings. Each of those floors has eight sleeping bays (two on each of the four sides of the building), for a total of 24 bays per building. Table 4.7 summarizes our assessment of Option Five.

Table 4.7. Option Five: Integrate Sleeping Bays

Degree to which option reflects working and housing conditions in the operational USAF	Does not simulate segregated sleeping and integrated working conditions in the operational USAF
Degree of integration across flight and trainees	Allows flights to be integrated all the time
Concerns over critical mass	Potential critical mass concerns if women are less than 15% of a flight
Impact on where BMT training occurs	Maintains training and mentoring time in sleeping bays
Impact on MTI model of instruction	• MTI team model could provide trainees with more role models and mentors, and MTIs with more leadership opportunities • MTI team model may require an adjustment period
Impact on BMT scheduling	Could create more complex scheduling issues
Impact on BMT facilities	Facilities modifications required
Impact on BMT IT systems	Requires a change to IT systems used to assign and track trainees
Timeline for implementation	Longest timeline for implementation due to facilities changes
Associated costs	*Option 5.A: 50/50 Split without Changing Rooms:* $29,494 per bay/$707,856 per building Total: $4,247,136 (Six buildings) *Option 5.B: 50/50 Split with Changing Rooms:* $69,376 per bay/$1,667,856 per building Total: $10,007,136 (Six buildings) *Option 5.C: 75/25 Split with Changing Rooms:* $95,091 per bay/$2,282,184 per building Total: $13,693,104 (Six buildings)
Main Takeaways	• Biggest departure from current housing and training arrangements • Most expensive option and longest timeline due to facilities changes

NOTE: These costs include first-year personnel costs for the new MTI team model. This cost includes the addition of an assistant director of operations and the loss of one flight commander per squadron. If the loss of one flight commander per squadron is not offset by the addition of one assistant director of operations, the costs are $558,270. Required IT costs for these options are assumed to be captured in current contracts or already planned and programmed.

Assessment of Option Five

This option would be the biggest departure from current housing and training arrangements, but it would allow flights to be integrated all of the time. This option would also be the most expensive option and the one with the longest timeline because it would require modifications to current facilities. This option would maintain training and mentoring in the sleeping bays and would utilize the same MTI team model proposed in Options Two, Three, and Four. The implementation of this MTI model could take an adjustment period, but this model could provide trainees with more mentors and MTIs with more leadership opportunities.

Potential Costs

This option is the most expensive of the options because it requires modifications to existing facilities (see Table 4.7 for cost estimates). A detailed presentation of our cost analysis for this option can be found in Appendix B.

Key Takeaways

Option One will be the least disruptive to current BMT operations, will have the shortest timeline for implementation, and will achieve the smallest increase in GIT. Options Two and Three will increase GIT more than Option One, but less than Option Four. Option Four will increase GIT the most within the shortest timeline. Option Five is the greatest departure from current BMT policies and procedures and would have the longest implementation timeline.

As described above, each of the options also have different costs associated with them. Option One is the least expensive option because it does not require any modifications to facilities, nor does it require any additional personnel or changes to IT systems. Options Two, Three, and Four will have some costs associated with the implementation of the new MTI team model and some possible IT-related costs if changes to current systems are required very quickly. Option Five is the most expensive option because it requires modifications to facilities. Table 4.8 summarizes our assessment of the five GIT options.

Table 4.8. Summary of BMT Gender-Integration Options

	Option One: Integrate Select Training Activities	Option Two: Integrate Flights 50/50 After They Fall Out From Sleeping Bays	Option Three: Integrate Flights 50/50 in the Sleeping Bays After Morning Hygiene	Option Four: Integrate as Many Flights as Possible 25 Percent Women (75/25 Option)	Option Five: Integrate Sleeping Bays
Degree to which option reflects working and housing conditions in the operational USAF	• Simulates segregated sleeping conditions in the operational USAF • Only somewhat simulates integrated working conditions in the operational USAF	Most closely simulates segregated sleeping and integrated working conditions in the operational USAF	Does not simulate segregated sleeping and integrated working conditions in the operational USAF	Most closely resembles sleeping and working conditions in the operational USAF	Does not simulate segregated sleeping and integrated working conditions in the operational USAF
Degree of integration across flight and trainees	Increases GIT the least	• Fewer training flights could be gender-integrated than under Option Four • Flights that are integrated would experience very high levels of gender integration (50%)	• Fewer training flights could be gender-integrated than under Option Four • Flights that are integrated would experience very high levels of gender integration (50%)	Allows for larger proportion of flights and trainees to be integrated	Allows flights to be integrated all the time

	Option One: Integrate Select Training Activities	Option Two: Integrate Flights 50/50 After They Fall Out From Sleeping Bays	Option Three: Integrate Flights 50/50 in the Sleeping Bays After Morning Hygiene	Option Four: Integrate as Many Flights as Possible 25 Percent Women (75/25 Option)	Option Five: Integrate Sleeping Bays
Impact on where BMT training occurs	• Maintains the current gender-segregated flight structure • Maintains training and mentoring in sleeping bays	• Training and mentoring activities could be maintained in in sleeping bays or moved to other venues • Members of the same bay would also be members of different training flights; this could potentially cause confusion • Could pose challenges for standardization of training	• Maintains training and mentoring time in sleeping bays • Members of the same bay would also be members of different training flights; this could potentially cause confusion • Could pose challenges for standardization of training	• Training and mentoring activities could be maintained in sleeping bays or moved to other venues • Members of the same bay would also be members of different training flights; this could potentially cause confusion • Could pose challenges for standardization of training	Maintains training and mentoring time in sleeping bays
Impact on MTI model of instruction	No change to current MTI model of instruction	• MTI team model could provide trainees with more role models and mentors, and MTIs with more leadership opportunities • MTI team model may require an adjustment period	• MTI team model could provide trainees with more role models and mentors, and MTIs with more leadership opportunities • MTI team model may require an adjustment period	• MTI team model could provide trainees with more role models and mentors, and MTIs with more leadership opportunities • MTI team model may require an adjustment period	• MTI team model could provide trainees with more role models and mentors, and MTIs with more leadership opportunities • MTI team model may require an adjustment period
Impact on BMT scheduling	Does not require any scheduling or logistical changes	Could create more complex scheduling issues	Could create more complex scheduling issues	Could create more complex scheduling issues	Could create more complex scheduling issues
Impact on BMT facilities	No facilities modifications required	No facilities modifications required	No facilities modifications required	No facilities modifications required	Facilities modifications required
Impact on BMT	Does not	Requires a	Requires a	Requires a	Requires a

	Option One: Integrate Select Training Activities	Option Two: Integrate Flights 50/50 After They Fall Out From Sleeping Bays	Option Three: Integrate Flights 50/50 in the Sleeping Bays After Morning Hygiene	Option Four: Integrate as Many Flights as Possible 25 Percent Women (75/25 Option)	Option Five: Integrate Sleeping Bays
IT Systems	require any scheduling or logistical changes	change to IT systems used to assign and track trainees	change to IT systems used to assign and track trainees	change to IT systems used to assign and track trainees	change to IT systems used to assign and track trainees
Timeline for implementation	Shortest	Medium-term	Medium-term	Medium-term	Longest timeline due to facilities changes
Associated costs	None	$1,404,420[a]	$1,404,420[a]	$1,404,420[a]	***Option 5.A: 50/50 Split without Changing Rooms:*** $29,494 per bay/ $707,856 per building Total: $4,247,136 (Six buildings) ***Option 5.B: 50/50 Split with Changing Rooms:*** $69,376 per bay/ $1,667,856 per building Total: $10,007,136 (Six buildings) ***Option 5.C: 75/25 Split with Changing Rooms:*** $95,091 per bay/ $2,282,184 per building Total: $13,693,104 (Six buildings)

	Option One: Integrate Select Training Activities	Option Two: Integrate Flights 50/50 After They Fall Out From Sleeping Bays	Option Three: Integrate Flights 50/50 in the Sleeping Bays After Morning Hygiene	Option Four: Integrate as Many Flights as Possible 25 Percent Women (75/25 Option)	Option Five: Integrate Sleeping Bays
Main takeaways	• Increases GIT the least but has shortest timeline • Least disruptive and lowest cost option	• Fewer flights and trainees could be integrated than Option Four • Would require MTI team model, IT and scheduling changes • Maintains training and mentoring in sleeping bays	• Fewer flights and trainees could be integrated than Option Four • Would require MTI team model, IT and scheduling changes • Would be major departure from current housing and training arrangements	• Allows for more flights and trainees to be integrated than Options One, Two, and Three • GIT can be substantially increased fairly quickly and with modest costs • Maintains training and mentoring in sleeping bays	• Biggest departure from current housing and training arrangements • Most expensive option and longest timeline due to facilities changes

[a] These costs include first-year personnel costs for the new MTI team model. This cost includes the addition of an assistant director of operations and the loss of one flight commander per squadron. If the loss of one flight commander per squadron is not offset by the addition of one assistant director of operations, the costs are $558,270. Required IT costs for these options are assumed to be captured in current contracts or already planned and programmed.

Next, we turn to an analysis in which the RAND team applied historical BMT data to two of these options to predict both the proportion of training flights that would be integrated under each option and the proportion of trainees that would be integrated under each option.

5. Applying Historical BMT Data to Current Facility Constraints and GIT Options

Using historical BMT data (incoming class sizes, proportional male and female intake, and facility constraints), we examined how different GIT options would affect three outcome criteria: (1) the feasibility of the various GIT options in current facilities, (2) the proportion of training flights and individual trainees that could be integrated across various incoming class sizes, and (3) the number of women and male/female proportions within each training flight.

This analysis does not make recommendations on scheduling, incoming class sizes, or facility changes. Instead, it represents the most likely outcomes of GIT, given the current available information: known facility constraints and historical class sizes. This analysis can determine the feasibility of various GIT options, as well as how different options affect the proportion of integration across both training flights and individual trainees.

Facilities Constraints on Assigning Male and Female Trainees to Open Bays

Male and female trainees are currently housed in separate open-bay sleeping areas. The number of trainees in each bay is constrained by facility design and physical space. Currently, the open-bay sleeping areas include four rows of 13 beds and house a maximum of 52 trainees. To balance the efficient use of staff, trainee health, and the optimal use of the space, BMT administrators consider 42 to 52 trainees per sleeping bay to be optimal. The number of bays needed is determined by the size of the incoming class. Once male and female trainees are assigned to sleeping bays, they are then assigned and integrated into training flights.

Consider an incoming class of 1,000 total trainees (250 women and 750 men). This class would be assigned to 20 open bays to meet this capacity. The female trainees would be assigned to five bays of 50 trainees each, and the male trainees would be assigned to 15 different bays of 50 trainees each.

The historical data we used spans 173 incoming classes from October 1, 2012, to March 28, 2016 (average trainees per incoming class = 658, average male trainees per incoming class = 511, and average female trainees per incoming class = 147). Incoming classes varied in size, ranging from a minimum of 344 trainees to a maximum of 927 trainees; on average, each class had 659 incoming trainees. Female representation also varied (ranging from a minimum of 13 percent female trainees to a maximum of 29 percent female trainees, for an average of 22 percent female trainees per class).[1]

Translating Historical Incoming Class Sizes to Current Facility Constraints

The research team developed an optimization model to assign "historical" trainees to current training facilities.[2] An optimization model allows the user to alter multiple variables to identify the best outcome. In this case, the variables and constraints were provided by BMT administrators at Lackland AFB. This optimization model can be found in Appendix D.

In our model, open bays were initially constrained to 42 to 52 trainees (regardless of gender), but this constraint was too stringent. Of the 173 incoming classes, 75 (43 percent) could not be assigned to sleeping bays because small incoming classes of female trainees would either be too small (less than 42 trainees per bay) or too many (greater than 52 trainees per bay). In the most extreme historical example, one incoming class had only 68 female trainees.[3] Two bays of 34 female trainees are far below the minimum recommended by BMT administrators (42 trainees per bay), and one bay of 68 trainees is physically impossible based on current facility constraints.

When we relaxed the open-bay constraint by assigning as few as 34 female trainees to a sleeping bay,[4] an additional 62 of 173 (36 percent) incoming classes were able to be assigned to sleeping bays. By relaxing the original constraint on male sleeping bays, an additional ten of 173 (6 percent) incoming classes were assigned to sleeping bays. A single, exceedingly small incoming class—comprising 273 male trainees and 97 female trainees—could not be assigned to sleeping bays, even after relaxing these constraining parameters. For this incoming class to be assigned to sleeping bays, the female trainees were assigned to three bays, with 31 or 32 female trainees in each, and the male trainees were assigned to seven bays with 39 male trainees in each.

Applying Historical Data to GIT Options

Once the historical data was applied to current training facilities, the research team could then apply the historical data to different GIT options to assess their feasibility. This analysis explores two options for integrating training flights: Option Two (the 50/50 option) and Option Four (the 75/25 option). In both options, trainees would sleep in gender-segregated sleeping bays, and in the morning, they would intermix with another sleeping bay or bays to form an

---

[1] More recent data from incoming classes *after* April 1, 2016, were not included in the analysis, because these individuals did not yet complete BMT as of the time of this report, and therefore no attrition information was available.

[2] This optimization model can be found in Appendix D.

[3] The historical data provided by Lackland AFB indicated that this incoming class of 68 women was assigned to two different open bays with 34 female trainees each.

[4] This 34-bed lower limit was selected based on the historical minimum for the smallest loaded female open sleeping bay.

integrated training flight. Once the integrated training flights completed their training for the day, the training flights would disband and return to their respective male and female open bays.

The 50/50 option pairs one female sleeping bay with one male sleeping bay to form two integrated training flights. In this option, the remaining male bays cannot be matched with a female bay because of the larger number of male trainees. They do not integrate and form all-male training flights that correspond to their sleeping bay.

The 75/25 option proportionally groups a quarter of the women from a female bay with a quarter of the men from three male bays to form four integrated training flights with 25 percent women and 75 percent men in each training flight. In other words, male and female trainees sleep separately (one female bay and three male bays) and then integrate into four integrated training flights.

Feasibility of Options to Achieve Targeted Levels of Integration

Our analysis also explored the feasibility of both the 50/50 and 75/25 options and found that neither option could always achieve their targeted levels of integration. For instance, unless an incoming class is composed of 50 percent women, the 50/50 option can never pair male trainees with enough female trainees to integrate all training flights with 50 percent men and 50 percent women. The historical data indicate that at most, the 50/50 Option would be able to integrate 70 percent of its training flights as 50/50 flights, but this was very rare (only two of 173 incoming classes, 1 percent). Of 173 incoming classes, most (68 percent) would be able to integrate approximately half of their training flights (45–55 percent) as 50/50 flights.

Consequently, that also means that most incoming classes would not be able to integrate the remaining half of their training flights. Either as many integrated training flights of 50 percent male and 50 percent women are formed as possible (with remaining flights staying all male), or the proportion of female trainees needs to be dramatically adjusted to ensure that all training flights can be integrated. However, because there are always less than 50 percent women in incoming classes and trainees are integrated by bays (with bed constraints) rather than as individuals, this second strategy may offer little capacity to redistribute women further.

Our analysis also found that the 75/25 Option cannot always proportionally distribute 25 percent female trainees across all training flights. If the total number of flights in a new class is not divisible by four, even after adjusting the number of trainees in each sleeping bay as described earlier, other adjustments must be made. A small number of all-male flights need to be allowed, a small number of flights need to be integrated using the 50/50 concept, or the proportion of female trainees needs to be adjusted to ensure that all training flights are integrated, based on the number of women available in the incoming class flights. However, because trainees are integrated by bays (with bed constraints), rather than as individuals, this third strategy may offer little capacity to redistribute women further.

Based on historical data, the 75/25 option would be completely successful at proportionally integrating 25 percent female trainees into each training flight for 69 of the 173 incoming classes (40 percent). Eighty-two new classes (47 percent) would require at least one all-male training flight, and 22 incoming classes (13 percent) would require some kind of other modification (e.g., a 50/50 pairing of male and female bays or a modification to the proportion of women in each flight) to form integrated training flights.

Degree of Gender Integration Across Training Flights and Across Trainees

Gender integration occurs at both the training flight level and the individual level. To illustrate the degree of gender integration for incoming classes, we examined both the proportion of GIT flights under the two options and the proportion of trainees in GIT flights under the two options. The 173 new classes in the historical data generated 2,538 training flights.

As indicated in Figure 5.1, by pairing one male bay and one female bay using the 50/50 option, 1,188 of the 2,538 training flights (47 percent) would be integrated and 1,350 training flights (53 percent) would be all male. In addition, 48 percent of all trainees in the historical data would participate in GIT flights.

As indicated in Figure 5.1, the modified 75/25 option (in which a small number of all-male flights need to be allowed, a small number of flights need to be integrated using the 50/50 concept in concert with the 75/25 option, or the proportion of female trainees is adjusted) resulted in 2,376 integrated training flights (94 percent) of the 2,538 total. With this approach, 92 percent of all trainees would participate in integrated training flights.

Figure 5.1. Examining the Proportion of Gender Integration in 50/50 and Modified 75/25 Options

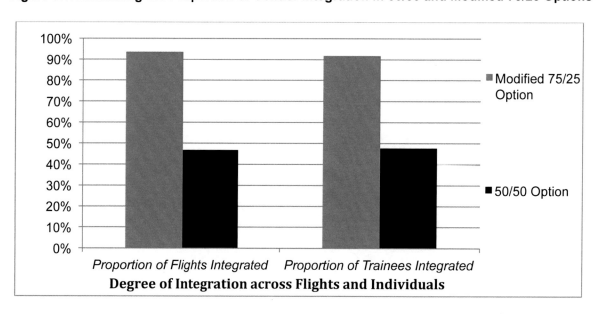

SOURCE: RAND analysis of U.S. Air Force Air Education and Training Command, 2016.
NOTE: N = 2,538 training flights across three-year historical sample.

Conclusions

Our analysis of the historical data explored the feasibility of both the 50/50 and 75/25 options and found that neither option could always achieve their targeted levels of integration. The historical data indicate that of 173 incoming classes, most (68 percent) would be able to integrate approximately half of their training flights (45–55 percent) as 50/50 flights. Consequently, most incoming classes would be unable to integrate the remaining half of their training flights.

Our analysis of the historical data also found that the 75/25 option cannot always proportionally distribute 25 percent female trainees across all training flights. Based on historical data, the 75/25 option would be completely successful at proportionally integrating 25 percent female trainees into each training flight 40 percent of the time. The remainder of the flights would need to be all-male flights or 50/50 flights, or the proportion of women in each flight would need to be changed.

Using the 50/50 option, 47 percent of training flights would be integrated, and 48 percent of all trainees in the historical data would participate in GIT flights. Using the modified 75/25 option, 94 percent of training flights would be integrated, and 92 percent of all trainees would participate in GIT flights.

Based on these analyses, the modified 75/25 option offers the greatest degree of integration. It offers a higher proportion of integrated training flights and more total trainees in integrated flights than the 50/50 option. The 50/50 option would allow fewer than half of the training flights to be integrated and fewer than half of incoming trainees to participate in GIT.

6. The Effects of Attrition on GIT Options

Many studies propose that a critical mass—the minimum minority representation within a group (in this case, women)—can facilitate successful performance outcomes for that minority group. However, there is a great deal of disagreement among experts as to whether or not the concept of a critical mass is valid and if so, what the minimum threshold is in specific contexts. Nevertheless, some researchers assert that when very small numbers of minorities (one or two) are in a group, their performance declines (Lord and Saenz, 1985, p. 918; Sekaquaptewa and Thompson, 2003, pp. 68–74; Richman, vanDellen, and Wood, 2011).

Given potential concerns regarding critical mass, we analyzed how attrition would affect female representation in both the 50/50 option and the 75/25 option [1] When distributed across all training flights, attrition could potentially reduce the number of women in a training flight to very low levels.

In this chapter, we examine what the literature on critical mass can and cannot tell us, and then we present our attrition analysis. Our analysis sets out to answer a series of questions.

1. How will attrition affect the proportion of women within an integrated training flight and the number of female trainees within GIT flights?
2. Will attrition change the proportion within GIT flights?
3. After attrition, how many female trainees will complete BMT in each training flight?

This analysis illustrates how various constraints and different GIT options impact the number of women likely to complete BMT in each training flight.

Findings from the Literature on Critical Mass

Critical mass refers to the idea that experiences in a minority status change as the minority group's numbers increase.[2] A minimum threshold of women in a group may alleviate many challenges associated with gender integration. However, as is indicated by the literature as well as the experiences of foreign militaries, the exact critical mass proportion or threshold that might alleviate gender-integration challenges is unclear.

Most of the literature on critical mass focuses on civilian contexts, such as legislatures and other civilian workplaces; therefore, it is unclear to what extent these findings may be relevant to critical mass in BMT. However, the literature on critical mass does not agree on specific (or even

---

[1] There are numerous ways to operationalize attrition at BMT: recycled (held back) to be put into a new flight or completely separated from BMT. For the purposes of the present analysis, assigning male and female flight sizes, and direct concern regarding flight-level integration, attrition was operationalized as the loss of an individual from the flight regardless of the reason.

[2] The following review is a summary of the findings in Schaefer et al., 2015.

general) thresholds for what substantiates or constitutes a critical mass. The debate on the role of critical mass in gender dynamics can be traced back to a 1977 sociological study that claimed gender *proportions* influenced patterns of gender interaction. Rosabeth Moss Kanter argued that in *skewed* group types (groups in which there were "a large preponderance of one type over another"), women were subject to "the dynamics of tokenism" (Kanter, 1977, p. 966).[3] Kanter's study assumed that *skewed* groups became *tilted* groups[4] when the minority group comprised 15 to 35 percent of total group population. Twenty percentage points is a relatively wide margin, and the findings from other studies support the gap in agreed-upon tipping points. For example, one 2008 study of women on select *Fortune 1000* company corporate boards stated that 30-percent representation on corporate boards was the "magic number" that allowed for women's perspectives to impact boardroom decisions (Konrad et al., 2008, p. 148). A 2013 study of 151 corporate boards in Germany between 2000–2005 confirmed this number (Joecks et al., 2013). However, a 2001 study on women in the New Zealand parliament between 1975 and 1999 (a period in which the proportion of women in the New Zealand parliament grew from 4 to 29 percent) stated that at 15 percent of the parliamentary population, female politicians were more actively involved in debates on childcare and parental leave, but even at 30 percent of the parliamentary population, women proved unable to significantly alter parliamentary culture or policy decisions (Grey, 2001, p. 15).

Despite a substantial literature asserting and examining the benefits of critical masses of women within groups, critical mass theory is "increasingly rejected as an explanatory theory of women's substantive representation."[5] In fact, a reoccurring theme within the critical mass literature is the complete rejection of the idea that gender proportions, in and of themselves, influence patterns of gender interactions. In most cases, these authors point out that the mechanisms by which critical mass produces a change in the status or employment conditions of women are not specified.[6]

Findings Regarding Solo Women in a Group

However, a considerable amount of research has examined the effects of one extreme—being the only woman in a group. The majority of this research indicates that women in solo status positions in groups draw more attention from the rest of the group, which is associated with

---

[3] Tokenism is viewed as bringing on a variety of issues, including sexual harassment, performance pressures, role entrapment, and self-distortion; these factors collectively put women at a competitive disadvantage within the organization, decreasing their performance and asserting dominant-group solidarity (Kanter, 1977, pp. 969–977).

[4] *Tilted* groups have "less extreme distributions and less exaggerated effects . . . with a ratio perhaps 65:35" (Kanter, 1977, p. 966).

[5] Studies on the benefits of critical mass include Kanter, 1977; Childs and Krook, 2008; Konrad, Kramer, and Erkut, 2008; Joecks, Pull, and Vetter, 2013; Rosen and Martin, 1998; Hagedorn et al., 2007; and Torchia, Clabro, and Huse, 2011. Quote from Childs, Webb, and Marthaler, 2010.

[6] See Martin, Harrison, and Dinitto, 1983; Zimmer, 1988; Yoder, 1991; Grey, 2001; Beckwith and Cowell-Meyers, 2007; Caiazza, 2004; Poggione, 2004; Childs and Krook, 2008; and Chaney, 2006.

decreases in performance (Lord and Saenz, 1985, p. 918; Sekaquaptewa and Thompson, 2003, pp. 68–74). Research with civilians also suggests that the presence of multiple women in a group reduces this effect and provides social support that can increase performance and resilience (Richman, vanDellen, and Wood, 2011).

A 1990 report by the Women's Research and Education Institute concurred more generally with Kanter, stating that:

> as long as women constitute small numbers in nontraditional employment contexts, substantial obstacles will remain. The presence of a few token women may do little to alter underlying stereotypes, and the pressure placed on such individuals makes successful performance less likely (Rix, 1990, p. 185).

Konrad et al.'s 2008 study of corporate boards reinforced Kanter's findings and stated that "lone women," or *solos*, reported feeling invisible or overly visible, having to play catch-up, having to break stereotypes, and difficulties in having their voices heard—all of which reduced their capacity to contribute (Konrad et al., 2008, pp. 145–151). The adverse effects of skewed groups were also present in the construction professions, wherein women made up less than 5 percent of the total workforce (including the managerial levels of the industry) and faced occupational isolation and limited promotion prospects (Greed, 2000).

More recent studies counter the notion that skewed groups or even solo status adversely affect female performance. For instance, in a 2011 study of American corporate board members, the narrative of the detrimental stresses of being the first and only woman was at odds with many female board members' embrace of their "pathbreaker" status and the benefits they perceived accompanying this status (Broome et al., 2011, p. 1051).

Critical Mass in the U.S. Military and Foreign Militaries

Existing U.S. military personnel policies provide very little in terms of specific guidance on using or assuring critical mass. Indeed, a survey of 14 USAF, Army, USMC, and Navy regulations relating to the assignment of female personnel reveals a dearth of critical mass concepts (Schaefer et al., 2015). In fact, the only service regulation stating *minimum* numbers of women assigned to particular units is a 2011 Navy regulation stating that a minimum of one female officer and one female chief petty officer will be assigned to all gender-integrated ships and squadrons.[7]

A few studies have examined critical mass in the U.S. military. For instance, early research on critical mass found that Army work groups with a higher percentage of women were less cohesive than those with fewer women (Rosen et al., 1996).[8] However, later research found that

---

[7] See U.S. Department of the Navy, Office of the Chief of Naval Operations, 2011. At the same time, however, this regulation rejected thresholds by stating the "gender mix of any given work center will *not* be a consideration in the assignment of women," (p. 5), emphasis added.

[8] The percentage of women in the groups ranged from less than 1 percent to 59 percent.

a higher proportion of women in Army work groups was associated with higher levels of perceived acceptance by those women (Rosen and Martin, 1998).[9]

Several studies of foreign militaries suggest that solo status for women in the military has negative effects. For instance, the Norwegian military has found that women assigned as solos are less satisfied with their jobs and tend to leave their units within a year because they feel isolated and that they do not fit in (Schaefer et al., 2015). A study of female officers in gender-integrated Israeli Defense Force units found that solo status female officers in the unit had lower performance ratings than male officers in the unit, whereas women in units with higher proportions of women had better performance ratings than men in the unit (Pazy and Oron, 2001).

There is even less information available about the number or proportion of women that actually constitutes a critical mass, and different countries have pursued different strategies on this issue. The Norwegian military, for example, has a target that the military will be 20-percent women, but it did not conduct any formal analysis to establish that target, and the target has not been reached.[10] In Canada, the use of a critical mass approach was used to assess the likely effects of integrating women into some occupations in 1987 (prior to their full integration). Initially, the critical mass approach meant that women could not be assigned in groups smaller than ten to training programs and operational units (Davis, 2014). Later, this threshold was revised so that the target for women in the Army in general, and in combat arms training courses and units specifically, was 25 percent. Finally, in Australia, the critical mass approach has been balanced against a desire to spread women evenly throughout the force.

Effects of Attrition on Gender Proportion in Integrated Training Flights

In order to identify how differences in attrition could change the proportion of women within integrated training flights, the research team applied attrition rates to the number of male and female trainees within training flights across the 50/50 and 75/25 options. According to historical data from BMT administrators, male and female trainees attrite at different rates (10 percent overall, 9 percent for male trainees, and 14 percent for female trainees). Using the historical data, the research team calculated the average number of men and women within training flights. To estimate how many trainees will attrite, the numbers of male and female trainees within training flights were multiplied by these attrition rates. These trainees were then subtracted from their training flights to reflect attrition. Finally, the research team calculated the average proportion of female trainees remaining within training flights. This was calculated separately for the 50/50 and 75/25 options.

---

[9] In this study, the percentage of women in each group ranged from 2 percent to 48 percent.

[10] Norwegian military researchers note that if the percentage of women in the military is below this number, women tend to be isolated; it may take as much as 40 to 60 percent women to fully achieve integration and to avoid many of the challenges faced by women when they make up a smaller percentage of the force (Schaefer et al., 2015).

As indicated in Figure 6.1, on average, attrition by gender did not appear to affect the proportion of women within integrated training flights. This was true for both the 50/50 option and the 75/25 option. In the 50/50 option, the proportion of women within training flights dropped from 47 percent to 46 percent. In the 75/25 option, the proportion of women within training flights dropped from 25 percent to 24 percent.

Figure 6.1. Female Proportion of Training Flights Pre- and Post-Attrition in 50/50 and 75/25 Options

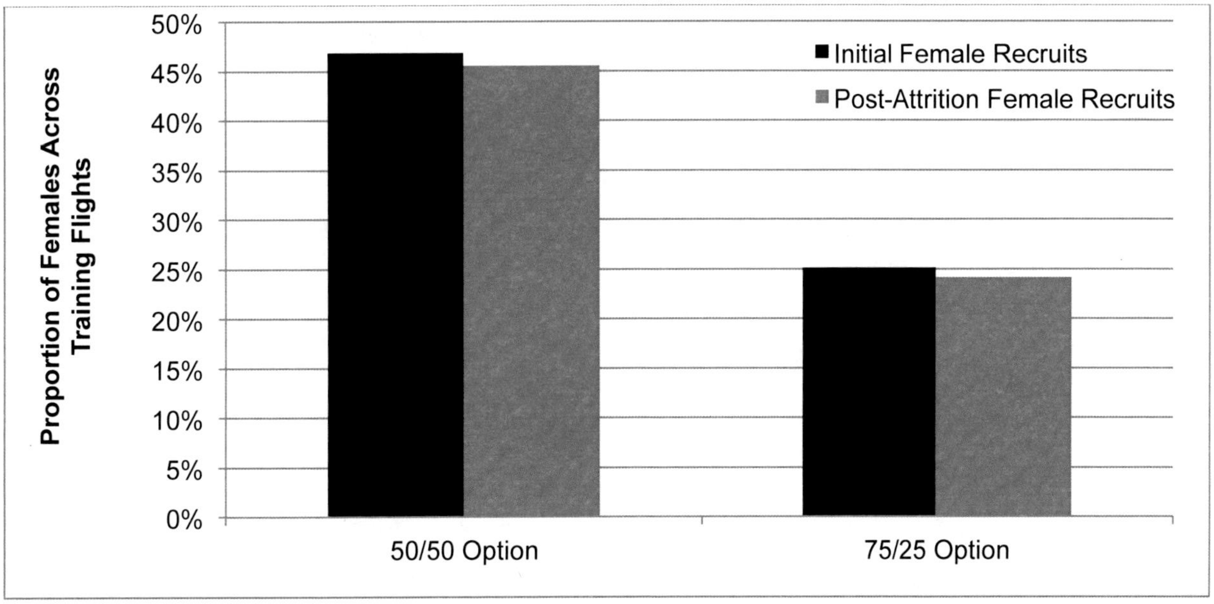

SOURCE: RAND analysis of U.S. Air Force Air Education and Training Command, 2016.
NOTE: N = 2,538 training flights across three-year historical sample.

These results only consider proportions, rather than the number of female trainees remaining within a training flight after taking into account attrition. Next, we consider how GIT and attrition affect how many female trainees will complete BMT within a training flight after taking into account attrition.

Effects of Attrition on Number of Female Trainees in Integrated Training Flights

After applying the historical attrition data to the GIT options, it is clear that attrition does not have a dramatic effect on the average number of women within training flights. Even at high attrition rates, the 50/50 option would still graduate 17 women in training flights, on average, and the 75/25 option would graduate eight women in training flights, on average (see Table 6.1).

Table 6.1. Estimated Effects of Attrition on Final Number of Women in Integrated Flights in 50/50 and 75/25 Options

	Average Number of Women in Flights		Smallest Number of Female Trainees in Flights		Largest Number of Female Trainees in Flights	
	50/50 Option	75/25 Option	50/50 Option	75/25 Option	50/50 Option	75/25 Option
Initial Flight Size	21	10	16	8	26	13
Very High Attrition (–21% rate)	17	8	12	6	20	10
High Attrition (–17% rate)	17	8	13	6	21	10
Average Attrition (–14% rate)	18	9	13	6	22	11
Low Attrition (–10% rate)	19	9	14	7	23	11
Very Low Attrition (–7% rate)	20	10	14	7	24	12

SOURCE: U.S. Air Force Air Education and Training Command, 2016.
NOTE: N = 2,538 training flights across three-year historical sample.
[a] Female attrition standard deviation = 3.47%. Low and very low attrition were estimated as one and two standard deviations below the mean rate of historical attrition, respectively. Similarly, high and very high attrition were calculated as one and two standard deviations above the mean rate of historical attrition, respectively.

To provide a range of extreme possibilities in the historical data, attrition rates were also applied to the smallest number of women in a training flight and the largest number of women within a training flight. As indicated in Table 6.1, even with the fewest female trainees, attrition still does not appear problematic in either option. In the training flight with the fewest female trainees coupled with the highest attrition, the 50/50 option would graduate 12 female trainees, and the 75/25 option would still graduate six female trainees. It is unlikely that either of these GIT options would result in the small numbers that the critical mass literature indicates may be problematic.

Effects of Attrition on Different Proportions of Female Integration

In case the USAF chooses to integrate all flights at some point, we also wanted to examine what kinds of effects attrition would have on different proportions of female integration. If female representation in a class is extremely small, and if these women are distributed across a large number of integrated training flights, the impact of attrition could be significant. Therefore, we next examined if integrating training flights with different proportions of female trainees might be exacerbated by attrition.

Table 6.2 examines different attrition rates and their impact on integrated training flights. Based on this analysis, it appears that integrated training flights with as high as a 15 percent proportion of female trainees will only graduate four or five women per training flight. Integrated training flights with less than 10 percent proportion of women will graduate only one or two women per training flight. Based on the historical incoming class data, training flights integrated with such small proportions of female trainees are unlikely. However, when these situations do occur, decisionmakers should consider the possibility that after attrition, only a single female trainee within a training flight may graduate; if that happens, it could have detrimental effects on critical mass.

Table 6.2. Estimated Effects of Attrition on Integrated Training Flights with Different Proportions of Women

Proportion of Female Integration in Training Flights	Initial Number of Female Trainees within Integrated Training Flights	Final Number of Women in Training Flight Post-Attrition				
		Very Low Attrition	Low Attrition	Average Attrition	High Attrition	Very High Attrition
5%	1	1	1	1	1	1
10%	3	3	3	3	3	2
15%	5	5	5	5	4	4
20%	8	7	7	7	6	6
25%	10	10	9	9	8	8
30%	13	12	11	11	10	10

Conclusions

The analyses in this chapter examined 173 incoming BMT classes spanning three years and explored extreme cases of low female representation and extreme attrition rates. The research literature does not present a clear minimum threshold for critical mass. Likewise, these analyses do not present a clear minimum threshold for how many female trainees within an integrated training flight will ensure their success. However, these results do provide a prediction of how many and what proportion of female trainees will complete integrated training based on different proportions of integration.

Using the 75/25 option, training flights would, on average, complete BMT with approximately ten female trainees within a 41-person training flight. If a training flight had historical minimums of women and high attrition, as few as approximately six female trainees might graduate.

Using the 50/50 option, training flights would, on average, complete BMT with approximately 19 female trainees within a 41-person training flight. If a training flight had historical minimums of women and high attrition, as few as approximately 13 female trainees would graduate.

Neither the 50/50 nor 75/25 options warrant concerns over lone women being assigned to training flights. Nevertheless, if the USAF decides to integrate all fights and extreme proportions are observed in an integrated training flight, our analyses indicate that integration proportions below 15 percent may risk graduating integrated training flights with only four or five women. Training flights that are below 10 percent female risk graduating a single female. Although female trainees made up 22 percent of incoming classes on average, the minimum incoming class was as low as 13 percent female. When an incoming class with a lower proportion of female trainees occurs, it seems prudent to assign more female trainees to fewer training flights.

7. Considerations When Implementing GIT

As we discussed in the previous chapters, GIT is not a singular policy or practice, nor does it aim to produce a singular training outcome. Instead, GIT comprises a diverse collection of possible changes in policies and practices that can affect a variety of BMT outcomes. Since GIT is fundamentally a complex organizational change process, USAF senior leaders should consider several critical issues when implementing GIT. In this chapter, we identify lessons from the literature on implementing organizational change and implementation lessons from foreign militaries. Being familiar with these issues and results from these studies will enable USAF senior leaders to communicate and motivate the required changes, anticipate potential challenges, prepare all stakeholders for the organizational change, and implement effective practices.

Lessons from the Literature on Implementing Organizational Change

As the USAF considers increasing GIT in BMT, there are lessons identified in the broad body of literature on organizational change and organizational change management that could facilitate this change. In particular, the literature identifies useful models of organizational change; barriers to organizational change; how those barriers can be overcome; and common errors in implementing organizational change. These streams of literature provide important guideposts for the USAF in its implementation of GIT.

Organizational Change Models

There are a variety of process models in the literature that try to identify the different phases of organizational change.[1] One of the most prominent models was developed by John Kotter in his book *A Force for Change* (1990). Kotter's change phase model consists of eight critical phases of change that should be implemented in the following sequence.

1. Establish a sense of urgency.
2. Create a coalition.
3. Develop a clear vision.
4. Share the vision.
5. Empower people to clear obstacles.
6. Secure short wins.
7. Consolidate and keep moving.
8. Anchor the change in the organizational culture.

---

[1] See Beckhard and Harris, 1987; Burke and Litwin, 1992, pp. 523–545; Grobman, 2005, pp. 350–382; and Van De Ven and Poole, 1995, pp. 510–540.

Cummings and Worley (1993) describe a five-phase general process for managing change that has a very similar structure.

1. Motivate change.
2. Create vision.
3. Develop political support.
4. Manage transition.
5. Sustain momentum.

Peter deLeon (1999) argues that policy innovation can be conceived as moving through six stages:

1. setting
2. adoption
3. early implementation
4. execution
5. evaluation and modification
6. implementation to completion.

Termination of the change process can occur at any point.

In addition to the change phase models mentioned above, two other prescriptive models of organizational change emerge from the literature, including bottom-up models of organizational change and top-down models of organizational change. We provide a brief overview of these prescriptive models below.

Bottom-Up Models of Organizational Change

Bottom-up theories of organizational change focus on the role that rank-and-file members of an organization play in bringing about organizational change.[2] The literature argues that bottom-up theories of organizational change can be more successful and easier to implement; the assumption is that since the ideas for change are generated from below, it will be easier for management to acquire the buy-in of the rank-and-file (Sabatier, 1986). The emphasis on bottom-up theories of organizational change has evolved into an emphasis in the literature on decentralized organizations. Decentralized organizations by definition are flatter, less-hierarchical organizations, and advocates of decentralized organizations argue that decentralized organizations are more adaptive and responsive to changing environments than hierarchical organizations (Brafman and Beckstrom, 2006).

Top-Down Models of Organizational Change

Unlike bottom-up models of organizational change that emphasize grassroots mobilization for organizational change, top-down models of organizational change argue that successful organizational change is imposed from upper management down to the rank-and-file. One of the

---

[2] See Sabatier, 1986, pp. 21–48; Lipsky, 1980; Hjern and Porter, 1981, pp. 211–227; Mechanic, 1962, pp. 349–364; and Moon, 2008.

most important strategies for implementing organizational change is to enlist the support of a high-level manager or "change agent" to fight for and protect efforts associated with organizational change (Lambright, 2008; Fernandez and Rainey, 2006). Such change agents often spur efforts for transformative change in an organization, and the most important function of a change agent is to support and fight for organizational change. [3]

However, not all who set out to become change agents succeed in changing an organization. Fernandez and Rainey (2006) argue that successful change agents pay particular attention to the following eight factors.

1. Ensure the need for change.
2. Provide a plan for change.
3. Build internal support for change and overcome resistance.
4. Ensure top-management support and commitment to the change.
5. Build external support for the change.
6. Provide resources for the change.
7. Institutionalize change.
8. Pursue comprehensive change.

Barriers to Organizational Change

Efforts to change organizations often fail because either the organizational culture or individuals in the organization are resistant to change (Beckhard and Harris, 1987). The broader literature identifies the following individual sources of resistance: fear of the unknown; self-interest; habit; personality conflicts; differing perceptions; general mistrust; and social disruptions. The broader literature also identifies the following organizational sources of resistance: structural inertia; bureaucratic inertia; group norms; a resistant organizational culture; threatened power; threatened expertise; and threatened resource allocation.

Overcoming Barriers to Organizational Change

Change agents have to find ways for the organizational culture to accept change as less frightening than stability. The literature on organizational change identifies, among others, the following means to deal with resistance to change: gradualism; education and communication; participation and involvement; negotiation and agreement; burden sharing; manipulation and co-option; explicit and implicit coercion; divide and conquer; and buy-out (Holt et al., 2007). Seen as a milestone in the field, Beckhard and Harris (1987) argued that all three of the following components must be present to overcome the resistance to change in an organization: dissatisfaction with the present situation; vision of what is possible in the future; and achievable first steps towards reaching this vision.

---

[3] See Jones, 2006, pp. 355–376; Pascale and Sternin, 2005; and Costa, de Matos, and Cunha, 2003.

Gender Integration Implementation Lessons and Policies from Foreign Militaries

Based on previous RAND research, we also identified several implementation lessons from the gender integration experiences of foreign militaries and the policies that they put into place to facilitate integration. These include: (1) the importance of leadership commitment and accountability, (2) phased implementation, (3) gender advisers, and (4) gender training programs. Each of these is discussed below.

The Importance of Leadership Commitment and Accountability

The first set of lessons from foreign militaries has to do with the importance of leadership commitment and accountability. According to senior leaders and key stakeholders in the integration process, without commitment and visible involvement by senior leaders, progress on integration is difficult or impossible to achieve. Integration needs to be supported by policy changes, and senior leaders are uniquely positioned to implement and enforce these types of changes.

Phased Implementation

According to opinions and observations of foreign military leaders and researchers, phased integration (in which integration occurs within a specific set of occupations or units before being gradually expanded to all units and occupations) often appears to support progress, as it allows integration to occur gradually alongside training. It also facilitates frequent status checks and course corrections as needed. Having a clear implementation plan is another key element of integration programs that have been more successful.

It is important to note that there is the question whether a gradual approach is more or less effective than one that implements integration at once. On one hand, a gradual approach allows for course correction and may spread out any negative implications of any changes over time, allowing for necessary adaptation. On the other, a phased approach may be too slow and runs the risk of starting a process that is never completed.

Gender Advisers

Gender advisers are positions specifically designated to advise leadership on issues related to gender (including lesbian, gay, bisexual, and transgender issues). These should be thought of as separate and distinct from a gender-integration oversight board, as the gender adviser positions are full-time advisers whose roles are to advise leadership on the day-to-day aspects of gender integration. Although gender advisers may be involved in periodic assessments conducted by the oversight board, they will have a distinct function. Gender advisers can operate at all levels and have been used in Norway, Sweden, Bulgaria, South Africa, and other countries. For example,

Sweden has relied on gender coaches and field advisers at various levels—from senior leadership to individual unit commanders (Egnell, Hojem, and Berts, 2012).

The USAF could consider the creation of a gender adviser to assist BMT commanders and MTIs with GIT-related issues, or assign a chief diversity officer who is trained in a range of diversity issues, including gender. These gender advisers could serve as subject-matter experts who advise BMT leadership, commanders, and MTIs on gender-related issues. This type of position may be especially helpful to leadership, commanders, and MTIs during the early phase of implementation as questions arise with the implementation of new policies. This position may also be helpful in the concurrent implementation of new transgender personnel policies.

Gender Training Programs

Previous research indicates that different foreign militaries have training programs that educate their force on gender issues (Schaefer et al., 2015). Some countries have specific gender training, some integrate this training into basic and refresher courses for all personnel, and some have special leadership training. In some cases, gender training is really "diversity training," while in others, it focuses specifically on gender issues. The same trainers who teach other BMT instructor courses could teach such gender-training courses, or external organizations or the gender coaches and advisers described above could teach these courses. By trying several different approaches and then surveying those who took each type of training about attitudes, both immediately after the training and periodically afterwards, the USAF could determine which approach is most effective.

8. Developing a Framework for Monitoring GIT in BMT

As we discussed in the previous chapter, the implementation of GIT can affect multiple policies, practices, and outcomes of BMT. In this chapter, we outline our approach to a framework to monitor the implementation of GIT. We identify issues, metrics, and data collection methods that the monitoring framework should track. Successful implementation of GIT requires that the USAF develop and continuously maintain a robust monitoring framework and periodically evaluate the impact of policy changes on strategic goals of BMT. It is important to note that data collection efforts and implementation monitoring efforts are essentially linked. Data collected for the monitoring framework provides the necessary foundation for the required evaluations. At the same time, the findings from the evaluation studies will inevitably suggest new data elements for the monitoring framework. To assist the USAF with these essential efforts, in this chapter, we outline elements of a data collection and monitoring framework and describe key characteristics of rigorous evaluation. The full monitoring framework can be found in Appendix C of this report.

Our Approach to a Monitoring Framework

Following a study of gender integration of the USMC infantry (Schaefer et al., 2015), we organize the issues and metrics for our monitoring framework using categories from the Doctrine, Organization, Training, Material, Leadership and Education, Personnel, Facilities, and Policy (DOTMLPF-P) structure and an additional category termed *attitudinal,* which includes well-being, welfare, morale, and misconduct. We also include types of issues ("what are you measuring?"), metrics ("how are you measuring progress, and what information do you need?"), and methods ("how are you collecting the information that you need to measure progress?"). In general, the metrics are designed to offer suggestions for ways to track and evaluate those issues that will be monitored; however, there are several different ways to measure progress on GIT. We also present several different methods for collecting data and discuss the value of considering a variety of methods to measure different aspects of GIT.

We used an iterative process to develop the list of issues to monitor. First, we produced an initial list of issues designed to cover a variety of policies and practices in all stages of BMT. These items included training curriculum material, as well as observations collected from the site visits across the U.S. military services. As the research team learned more about the policies and procedures used for GIT across the services, the research team refined these items over the course of each visit. In addition, we reviewed existing literature on GIT in the services and foreign militaries.

The issues in the monitoring framework cover both operational policies and practices, as well as strategic outcomes of BMT. The operational issues we considered include:

- decisions required to enact effective GIT, such as changes to training (e.g., degree of integration across training activities)
- training for MTIs (e.g., cross-training MTIs across male/female regulations)
- staffing of MTIs across integrated and nonintegrated flights (e.g., gender matching between MTIs with flights)
- rules and regulations regarding facilities
- expected levels of fraternization between genders.

In addition, we also consider possible impacts that the implementation of GIT could have on strategic objectives of BMT. We define strategic objectives of BMT as

- developing trainees to a level of physical fitness necessary for an airman
- instilling in trainees an understanding of the knowledge necessary for an airman
- socializing trainees into the values of the USAF
- ensuring trainees can complete this training in a safe environment.

In addition, this monitoring plan is also broken into two phases: the planning phase (before the decision whether or not to increase GIT has been made) and the implementation phase (after the decision whether to increase GIT has been made). We recommend routine monitoring of the implementation process. However, we recommend that the USAF periodically conduct a comprehensive evaluation of the integration process to reevaluate monitoring priorities. We recommend that an initial evaluation be conducted about three years after implementation and then every five years. Regardless of the outcome of these evaluations, we also emphasize the need for long-term, sustained routine monitoring to identify potential problems quickly as they evolve over time.

In Table C.1 in Appendix C, we describe the suggested issues, metrics, and methods to be monitoring during the planning phase. In Table C.2 in Appendix C, we describe the suggested issues, metrics, and methods to be monitored during the implementation phase. The USAF should not consider this list of issues as complete. Instead, the USAF should consider the list as an initial list. As we stated above, the evaluation of the implementation of GIT will suggest additional issues that the USAF should monitor and additional data that should be collected.

Potential Data Sources for the Monitoring Framework

The USAF will need to assess whether it is already collecting the necessary data to monitor the implementation of GIT, or whether it will need to initiate new data collection efforts. The USAF can use multiple data sources to develop metrics for the issues in our monitoring plan. These data sources include administrative data sources and existing surveys, facilitating focus groups, and conducting interviews with stakeholders, including MTI and trainees. Some of the metrics are quantitative (including various counts of different incidents and rates), while some of the metrics are qualitative in nature.

Administrative data sources will serve as important data sources. For instance, BTMS, is the primary means for tracking airmen during BMT. BTMS produces an end-of-course report card that is given to technical training schools. Additionally, BTMS tracks a number of skill evaluations that trainees progress through during basic training. Given that these are pass/fail requirements, these materials are likely to be less useful for the present purposes. BTMS also tracks PT outcomes. The system tracks both raw and age- and gender-normed PT scores. PT scores include the initial PT scores, four-week final score, and six-week final score. BTMS also indirectly tracks injuries, even though specific injuries are not recorded within BTMS due to Health Insurance Portability and Accountability Act regulations. Additionally, BTMS records retest scores within open-ended fields, along with instructor's comments. Moreover, BTMS tracks academic outcomes, including performance on the end-of-course test given to all trainees. Finally, BTMS also tracks some biographical information, including educational background, age, ethnicity, and marital status. Alleged Misconduct Reports are also another data source that the USAF can use to develop needed metrics for the monitoring framework. MTIs and other training personnel prepare Alleged Misconduct Reports to report misconducts.

The USAF can also develop metrics using data from existing surveys. These surveys include the End of Course Survey, the BMT Random/Targeted Safety and Well-Being Survey, the Airmen's Week Surveys, the RAND Trainee Survey, and the RAND MTI Survey. The End of Course Survey includes items assessing basic trainees' perceptions of their MTI's core competencies, their attitudes towards training, and general well-being. This survey also includes items reflecting misconduct. The BMT Random/Targeted Safety and Well-Being Survey allows trainees and airmen to report positive as well as negative events throughout various weeks of training. The Airmen's Week Surveys collect attitudinal data from a random sample of airmen (approximately 10 percent). Finally, there are two RAND surveys designed to collect information from trainees and MTIs.[1] The RAND Trainee Survey assesses trainee experiences and related reporting behaviors for abuse and misconducts, while the RAND MTI Survey assesses MTIs' awareness of trainees experiencing abuse, their perceptions of the related squadron climate, their quality of life, job attitude, the work environment, and job stressors. Both of these surveys already provide vital data for monitoring the BMT environment.

Essential Elements of Effective Evaluation

Establishing and maintaining a monitoring framework is a necessary condition to secure success of GIT. But the monitoring framework alone is not sufficient for sustained success of GIT. For a sustained success, we recommend that the USAF periodically conduct a formal evaluation of GIT and its impacts on BMT. We recommend that an initial evaluation be conducted about three years after implementation and then every five years. A rigorous

---

[1] See Keller et al., 2015.

evaluation that uses valid and reliable research methods can give the USAF a formal assessment of the process and outcomes of GIT.

Evaluation Begins with a Logic Model

Effective evaluation efforts require a logic model that specifies how GIT should work conceptually to achieve the desired outcomes of BMT. Generally, a logic model is a one-page diagram depicting inputs, activities, outputs, short-term outcomes, and impact. In addition, a rigorous logic model also specifies key assumptions that senior leaders make during the implementation of GIT and identifies external factors that can alter the outcomes and impact of GIT. The value of the logic model is not limited to evaluation efforts. The logic model can play a critical role in strategic communication needed to motivate required changes and explain the conceptual issues behind the changes. Figure 8.1 shows a basic template of a logic model for GIT.

Figure 8.1. Logic Model Template for GIT

RESOURCES	ACTIVITIES	OUTPUTS	SHORT-TERM OUTCOMES	IMPACT (Long-term)
In order to carry out planned activities, we will need the following:	In order to accomplish our objectives for GIT, we need to do these activities:	We can monitor our activities by counting or recording these events or performance:	We expect our activities to lead to these changes:	We expect that GIT will eventually lead to these changes:
Assumptions:			External Factors:	

SOURCE: Adapted from the W. K. Kellogg Foundation Foundation Logic Model Development Guide, 2006.

There are three types of evaluation: formative evaluation, process evaluation, and outcome evaluation. Each evaluation type is designed to assess specific stages of the implementation of GIT. Formative evaluation will guide the USAF in its initial efforts to implement GIT and provide information to help sustain it. Process evaluation will assess GIT implementation and monitoring framework performance, and it will inform the USAF how to strengthen GIT. Finally, outcome evaluation will assess how GIT impacts the strategic outcomes of BMT. Figure

8.2 outlines how each of these three types of evaluation can assess the different stages of GIT implementation.

Figure 8.2. Overall Evaluation Plan Should Contain Three Types of Evaluation

Formative Evaluation	Process Evaluation	Outcome Evaluation
Initial program Information to help "form" and stabilize the program	Program description Program monitoring Quality assurance	Does the program work? Does the program achieve strategic objectives?

Formative Evaluation

In the beginning stage of the implementation of GIT, the USAF should conduct a formative evaluation to adjust and solve problems. The formative evaluation will assess whether GIT has been implemented as planned. There is no single accepted methodology for formative evaluation (Royse et al., 2015, p. 126). Agencies often conduct formative evaluations using an internal ad hoc committee composed of a representative group of stakeholders. For instance, the USAF can assign an ad hoc committee of headquarters staff and MTIs to conduct the formative evaluation. The committee can review new policies, interview staff, and facilitate focus groups of MTIs and trainees for feedback.

Process Evaluation

After the initial stage of the implementation of GIT, the USAF should conduct a process evaluation. The process evaluation assesses the consistency of implementation. The process evaluation team must ensure that the implementation of GIT is consistent with senior leaders' vision depicted in the logic model. The process evaluation team reviews and revises the BMT policies impacted by GIT and should lead the development and maintenance of the GIT monitoring framework. While the formative evaluation tends to be a single-episode evaluation, process evaluation should be an ongoing task that ensures the fidelity of the implementation of GIT (Royse et al., 2015, p. 136).

Outcome Evaluation

While formative and process evaluation efforts ensure that the implementation of GIT is consistent with senior leaders' policy vision, the outcome evaluation examines the effect of GIT on senior leaders' strategic outcomes for the implementation of GIT. Unlike formative and process evaluation, the outcome evaluation must follow a set of well-established rigorous procedures, designs, and methods, and an outcome evaluation team is usually an independent external group.

A rigorous outcome evaluation effort begins with a well-designed logic model that we described above. The logic model provides not only senior leaders' strategic objectives; it also illustrates how resources and activities associated with GIT conceptually link to specific outputs, as well as short-term and long-term outcomes.

Based on the logic model, the evaluation team must develop valid and reliable measurements that reflect the underlying concepts specified in the logic model. The outcome evaluation team needs to develop specific measures to capture readiness and cohesion that go beyond the BMT training outcomes. The measures should include attitudinal measures that are specifically designed for gender issues in a military training context, such as the Modern Sexism Scale[2] and survey items used to measure egalitarian views on military and attitudes toward standards of performance from the Naval Academy Survey on Attitudes (Durning, 1978, pp. 4, 569–588).

In addition to a well-designed logic model and scientifically valid and reliable measurements, the effective outcome evaluation must use a rigorous analytical design. As we discussed in Chapter Seven, existing studies that we reviewed examine gender differences on training outcomes, but gender differences in outcomes do not necessarily reflect the effect of GIT on leaders' strategic objectives for the implementation of GIT. In addition, a simple comparison of aggregate BMT outcomes before and after the implementation of GIT does not give a valid measure of the effect of GIT.

To estimate the effect of GIT, the analytical design must allow the evaluation team to compare the outcomes associated with a group of trainees who underwent BMT during or after the implementation of GIT with those from a similar group of trainees who underwent BMT before the implementation of GIT. It is critical for the outcome evaluation team to be able to identify two groups of trainees whose characteristics are similar except for their undergoing BMT before or during/after GIT changes.

There are a variety of other analytical designs available to the evaluation team, including observational and experimental designs. When the evaluation team uses observational design, the team collects data as the implementation of GIT unfolds. In contrast, the experimental design requires that the evaluation team systematically alters some features of the implementation of GIT. Hence, observational design is easiest to execute but provides limited information about the causal effect of GIT. The experimental research design is most difficult to execute but allows the evaluation team to estimate the causal effect of GIT.

---

[2] See Swim et al., 1995, pp. 68, 199–214; and Swim and Cohen, 1997, pp. 21, 103–118.

Key Takeaways

- Successful implementation of GIT requires that the USAF develops and continuously maintains a robust monitoring framework and periodically conducts a comprehensive evaluation of GIT and its impact on BMT strategic goals.
- Data collected for the monitoring framework can provide essential baseline data for the evaluation teams.
- The USAF should develop a logic model for GIT implementation. It should concisely summarize inputs, activities, outputs, short-term outcomes, and impacts of GIT. In addition, it should specify key assumptions and identify external factors that can alter the outcomes and impacts of GIT.
- The logic model can assist evaluation efforts and the strategic communication needed to motivate required changes and explain conceptual issues behind the changes.
- In the early stages of GIT implementation, the USAF should execute formative and process evaluation to ensure that the implementation is consistent with senior leaders' strategic vision and objectives. These two evaluation efforts can be executed by internal committees.
- Even before implementing GIT, the USAF should plan for the impact evaluation of GIT. This will allow the evaluation team to collect baseline data needed to compare with trainees who will undergo BMT after implementation of GIT.
- Coordinating with the impact evaluation team, the USAF should consider implementing GIT over a period of time in phases. This will enable the impact evaluation team to execute cost effective experimental design to estimate causal impact of GIT on BMT outcomes.
- A robust monitoring framework and repeated impact evaluations will facilitate the successful implementation of GIT.

9. Conclusions and Recommendations

This chapter discusses our main conclusions and our recommendations for planning and implementation. Our findings identified five main options for increasing GIT in BMT.

1. Integrate select training activities.
2. Integrate flights 50/50 after they fall out from sleeping bays.
3. Integrate flights 50/50 in the sleeping bays after morning hygiene.
4. Integrate as many flights as possible with 25 percent women.
5. Integrate sleeping bays.

Each of these options has associated costs, as well as other advantages and disadvantages (see Table S.1). Option One is the least expensive option, but it also increases GIT the least. Options Two and Three are associated with some additional personnel costs, but they would allow those flights that are integrated to be integrated at higher proportions (50 percent male/50 percent female). However, fewer flights would be integrated than under Option Four. Option Four has the same personnel costs as Options Two and Three and allows the most flights to be integrated most quickly. Option Five is the most expensive option, but it would allow flights to be integrated all the time. The following conclusions focus on the main findings from our detailed analysis of these options and the tradeoffs across them.

Conclusions

The following main conclusions arose from our analysis.

- The optimal option for GIT will depend on the USAF's priorities.
- The 50/50 and 75/25 options cannot achieve their targeted levels of integration 100 percent of the time.
- The 75/25 option offers the greatest degree of integration on the shortest timeline.
- None of the options are likely to produce critically few women (five or fewer) in training flights.
- The 737th's proposed MTI team model will facilitate GIT and increase leadership opportunities for MTIs.

Each of these is discussed in detail below.

Optimal Option for GIT will Depend on USAF Priorities

Our analyses found that there is a range of options for increasing GIT in BMT. Depending on what the USAF's priorities are, some options are better than others in achieving those priorities. For instance, if the USAF's priority is cost, Option One is the best option because it does not require modifications to facilities, does not require additional personnel, and does not require modification to current IT systems. If the USAF's priority is to maintain current and mentoring

79

activities in the sleeping bays, Options Three and Four are the best options. If the USAF's priority is integrating men and women as much as possible during BMT, Option Five is the best option.

50/50 and 75/25 Options Cannot Achieve Targeted Levels of Integration All the Time

Our analysis of historical BMT data explored the feasibility of the 50/50 and 75/25 options and found that none of them could achieve their targeted levels of integration 100 percent of the time. For instance, unless an incoming class is composed of 50 percent women, the 50/50 option can never pair male trainees with enough female trainees to integrate all training flights with 50 percent men and 50 percent women. The historical data indicate that at most, the 50/50 option would be able to integrate 70 percent of its training flights as 50/50 flights, but this would be rare. Of 173 incoming classes, most (68 percent) would be able to integrate approximately half of their training flights (45–55 percent) as 50/50 flights. This means that most incoming classes would not be able to integrate the remaining training flights.

Our analysis also found that the 75/25 option cannot always proportionally distribute 25 percent female trainees across all training flights. Based on historical data, the 75/25 option would be completely successful at proportionally integrating 25 percent of female trainees into each training flight for 69 of the 173 incoming classes (40 percent). Eighty-two new classes (47 percent) would require at least one all-male training flight, and 22 incoming classes (13 percent) would require pairing of male and female bays to form integrated training flights. However, if the 75/25 option is modified to allow for more flexibility in the proportions across flights, the level of integration can achieve integration across 94 percent of all flights and 92 percent of all trainees.

75/25 Option Offers the Most Integration on the Shortest Timeline

Our analysis of historical BMT data indicates that the 75/25 option offers the greatest degree of integration on the shortest timeline. It offers a higher proportion of integrated training flights and more total trainees in integrated flights than Options Two or Three. The 75/25 option is also among the less expensive options because it does not involve any changes to facilities.

Neither the 50/50 nor 75/25 Option Would Produce Critically Few Women in Training Flights

Neither the 50/50 nor the 75/25 option would lead to critically few women (below five women per training flight) in a flight after factoring in historical attrition rates. However, our analysis indicated that integration proportions below 15 percent may risk graduating integrated training flights with four or five women. Training flights below 10 percent proportions of women risk graduating a single woman. Therefore, when an incoming class with a lower proportion of female trainees occurs, it seems prudent to assign more female trainees to fewer training flights.

The 737th TRG's Proposed MTI Team Model Will Facilitate GIT and Increase Leadership Opportunities for MTIs

Our analysis indicates that the 737th TRG's proposed MTI team model would not only facilitate the implementation of GIT, but its structure also increases leadership opportunities for MTIs. This model is also reflective of the operational USAF, and the additional leadership roles offered by the 737th TRG's proposed MTI team model will help prepare MTIs for future positions across the USAF.

Recommendations for Planning and Implementation

The planning phase presents the USAF with a critical window of opportunity to develop integration strategies, plans and policies, as well as to put the necessary data systems in place to monitor GIT over time. Insights from the literatures on organizational change and the integration experiences of foreign militaries inform the following recommendations.

- Clarify and communicate the purpose of change.
- Build support for the change.
- Ensure top leadership support and commitment.
- Consider phased implementation.
- Develop a detailed implementation plan and assign accountability.
- Institute both internal and external oversight of implementation.
- Monitor GIT over time.
- Ensure lasting change.

Each of these recommendations is discussed in detail below.

Clarify and Communicate the Purpose of Change

Clarifying and communicating the purpose of any change in GIT in BMT will be key to the successful implementation of those changes. If the need for change has not been clearly articulated by leadership, stakeholders will continue to question whether any change is necessary, and the implementation process will stagnate. Leadership can facilitate the implementation process by clarifying the goals of any changes to GIT, providing a shared vision of the change and articulating a clear plan for implementation.

Build Support for the Change

The successful implementation of any proposed changes to GIT will rely on the support of internal stakeholders. One strategy for building such support is to identify internal "change agents" and strong proponents of the proposed changes. As the organizational change literature indicates, change agents can be key in ensuring the successful implementation of organizational change. Most importantly, change agents can provide the leadership necessary to develop a roadmap for institutionalizing GIT and oversee its implementation.

Given our discussions with MTIs, there are several individuals in the MTI corps who are willing to be change agents and see themselves as proponents for increasing GIT. These MTIs have already provided extremely valuable input into the planning process, and their continued involvement and feedback during the implementation process will be critical.

In addition, there are undoubtedly some stakeholders who are skeptical or outright opposed to any changes in GIT. It is important that these voices are heard during the planning process and that their concerns are considered in the decisionmaking process. One strategy to do that is to solicit their input before a decision is made. This could be done through focus groups, surveys, or other meetings between leadership and various stakeholders. If the voices of opposition do not feel like their concerns were factored into an initial decision regarding any changes to GIT, they could continue to resist any changes.

Ensure Top Leadership Support and Commitment

Lessons from both the experiences of foreign militaries and the organizational change literature indicate that major organizational change can rarely succeed without leadership support and commitment. If top leadership does not reinforce a decision with continued support and commitment, implementation is likely to flounder, and resistance may arise. This is especially true in a military setting, where leaders set the command climate and enforce good order and discipline. Senior leaders will also play a critical role in disseminating a consistent message about changes to GIT to both internal and external audiences. Leadership (at all levels of the chain of command) can set the tone for the organizational change and ensure that cohesion is not negatively affected by any changes.

Consider Phased Implementation

According to opinions and observations of foreign military leaders and researchers, phased integration (in which integration occurs gradually) often appears to support progress, as it allows integration to occur gradually alongside training. It also facilitates frequent status checks and course corrections as needed. A clear implementation plan is a key element of integration programs that have been more successful.

It is important to note that there is the question whether a gradual approach is more or less effective than one that implements integration at once. On one hand, a gradual approach allows for course correction and may spread out any negative implications of any changes over time, allowing for necessary adaptation. On the other, a phased approach may be too slow and creates the risk of starting a process that gets sidetracked.

Develop a Detailed Implementation Plan and Assign Accountability

The literature also indicates that the development of a detailed implementation plan is another key element of successful organizational change. Well-designed implementation plans that assign responsibility, identify risks, and outline mitigation strategies are particularly

82

effective in streamlining implementation. These types of plans clarify the goals of organizational change and identify the risks associated with the change, as well as the actions that the organization will need to take to mitigate those risks. It is also critical that the implementation plan assigns responsibility and accountability for the various element of implementation. Without such accountability, the implementation process can stagnate or atrophy all together. Developing such a plan will ensure that the USAF will be using the same guidance once a GIT decision is made.

Institute Both Internal and External Oversight of Implementation

Both internal and external oversight of the GIT process will be crucial in not only conducting the monitoring, but also in setting and defining requirements for longer-term progress. While internal monitoring helps ensure consistent attention and leadership commitment, external monitoring provides objectivity, transparency, and accountability.

Internal oversight can help ensure that various oversight initiatives are integrated and coherent and that leadership commitment to integration is apparent. At the same time, monitoring efforts should "trickle down," incorporating midlevel commanders and leaders to ensure that the oversight of GIT is consistent. While periodic reviews are valuable, monitoring of GIT on a constant basis is important because it keeps GIT as a priority, demonstrates leadership commitment, and helps keep the changes to GIT moving forward. An internal oversight board should have full support from top USAF leadership in its efforts. This will be a key aspect of consistency to execute and enforce the monitoring plan over the long term.

External oversight is also important, as external organizations can provide an objective assessment of integration progress (or lack thereof) and could play an important independent role in making recommendations. External reviews conducted by experts, former military personnel, and civilians provide objectivity and accountability that internal reviews sometimes lack. As a result, they can often be more powerful in diagnosing problems with the implementation process and promoting change where obstacles exist.

Monitor GIT over Time

The literature also indicates that monitoring is a key element to implementing organizational change over the long term. A strong monitoring plan relies on robust data systems that facilitate the necessary data collection to measure implementation progress. The USAF should consider which data systems are already in place to collect the appropriate data to monitor progress over time, and whether any new data systems are necessary.

The monitoring framework presented in Appendix C offers the USAF suggestions on which issues might be included in a monitoring plan, as well as how to measure progress on those issues and what type of data collection methods could be used. However, in order for a monitoring plan to be effective, it cannot be static. As data are collected and analyzed, new issues and measures may need to be added to or deleted from the monitoring plan.

Such monitoring also needs to be sustained. While periodic reviews are valuable, everyday, constant monitoring of implementation is important to identify any problems quickly so that adjustments can be made. In addition, sustained monitoring can help identify other key metrics that should be tracked over time.

Ensure Lasting Change

Lastly, the literature indicates that there are several things that leaders at all levels of the chain of command can do to ensure lasting change, including: (1) providing the resources necessary to sustain change, (2) modeling the way for change, and (3) institutionalizing change. Providing the necessary resources reinforces leadership commitment to the change and signals to the organization that the change remains a priority. As described in Chapter Seven, role modeling is a powerful strategy to facilitate the implementation of organizational change. MTIs could be critical role models during the implementation process, especially given the evidence that instructors can influence the degree to which trainees accept or reject GIT. By formally institutionalizing any changes through changes in policy and procedures, leaders can also ensure that any changes will be sustained when leaders change.

Closing Thoughts

Our analysis indicates that the USAF has a range of options to increase GIT in BMT. Any GIT changes will likely be an iterative process. As the USAF makes initial changes, it will learn what works well and what does not work so well and will adjust accordingly. By putting in place the data collection systems needed to track progress of GIT over time, the USAF can build the evidence base upon which it can make well-informed decisions during the implementation process and identify problems early so that they can be mitigated. The recommended implementation strategies discussed in this chapter also offer additional ways in which the USAF can facilitate the successful implementation of any changes made to GIT during BMT.

Appendix A: RAND Project Air Force BMT GIT Assessment Discussion Protocol

1. **Current Structure of Basic Training**
   A. Can you explain to us how basic training is currently designed, as well as which activities are gender-integrated and which are not?
   B. Can you tell us why those particular activities are gender-integrated and others are not?
   C. What was the evidence upon which the current structure of basic training is based?
   D. What is the goal of the current structure of basic training and how does gender-segregated training in some areas and GIT in others help to achieve that goal?
   E. What are the strengths/advantages of the current structure of basic training?
      a. Could these be potentially enhanced by changes to the percentage of GIT?
         i. If so, how?
      b. Could changes to the percentage of GIT potentially negatively impact the strengths/advantages of the current structure of basic training?
         i. If so, how?
   F. What are the weaknesses/disadvantages of the current structure of basic training?
      a. Could these be potentially improved by changes to the percentage of GIT?
         i. If so, how?
      b. Could changes to the percentage of GIT potentially negatively impact the weaknesses/disadvantages of the current structure of basic training?
         i. If so, how?
   G. Can you tell us how the current structure of basic training evolved over time and why it evolved as it did?
   H. Have any lessons been learned from past experiences with gender-integrated basic training?
      a. If so, what are those lessons?
   I. Have the experiences of other services influenced the current structure for basic training?
      a. If so, how and what has your service learned from the experiences of the other services?

2. **Options for Changing the Degree of GIT in BMT**
   A. What factors should the USAF consider if it changes the percentage of GIT in BMT and why?
   B. Given your experiences with BMT, how could the percentage of GIT could be increased in BMT?
      a. What are the easiest ways to increase the percentage of GIT?
      b. What are the least expensive ways to increase the percentage of GIT?
   C. Given your experiences with BMT, are there obstacles to fully gender-integrating BMT?
      a. If so, what are those challenges?
      b. Are there ways to overcome or mitigate those challenges?
         i. If so, what are they?

D. What activities would be most difficult to gender-integrate and why?
    a. Are there ways to overcome or mitigate those challenges?
        i. If so, what are they?
E. What are the most expensive barriers to increasing GIT?

3. Cost-Related Questions

A. Do you have data related to the cost of the current structure of basic training, including the cost element structure at the lowest possible level (i.e., what are all the elements (e.g., personnel, facilities, IT infrastructure, materials, etc.) that make up the cost of basic training)?

B. Do you have any historical data that tracked changes in the cost of basic training as the percentage of GIT changed over time?

C. Do you have any historical data that captures the cost to implement specific GIT initiatives?

D. Do you have estimates/proposed costs for GIT initiatives that may or may not have been implemented?

E. Do you have any data that tracks the costs of individual basic training activities?

F. Do you know of any sources that might have such data?

4. Other Data-Related Questions

A. Do you have data that could help us identify performance outcomes over time as the degree of GIT has changed?

Appendix B: Cost Methodology and Analysis of Options for Integrating Sleeping Bays

This appendix presents the methodology used for estimating the construction costs associated with the three options for integrating BMT sleeping bays, as well as the detailed changes and costs associated with each option for integrating BMT sleeping bays.

Methodology for Estimating Construction Costs

The RSMeans Square Foot Costs, an industry standard for estimating construction costs, was used to estimate the costs of the various modifications (RSMeans, 2015). The RSMeans databases are leveraged by the DoD's Unified Facilities Criteria pricing guide, which provides the standard for rough order of magnitude cost estimates for DoD facilities. The Unified Facilities Criteria pricing guide did not provide an adequate level of detail to cost specific construction activities for this project; therefore, the RSMeans was used to acquire the necessary detail. Costs were estimated by applying factors such as cost per square feet (e.g., installing walls) to square footage estimates or cost per item (e.g., door installation) to the number of estimated items. Once a base cost is calculated, factors are applied based on the RSMeans to account for contractor fees (e.g., general requirements, overhead, and profit) and architect fees. Finally, all costs are adjusted based on a location factor. Again, this factor, which takes into account the costs in San Antonio, Texas, relative to a base cost, is included in the RSMeans manual. It should be noted that all costs are in 2015 dollars; a marginal upward adjustment should be expected to account for inflation. We note that while the modifications are fairly minor, we cannot be certain that they are feasible and would meet applicable building codes. Additional costs may be incurred to ensure that modifications meet current codes. Finally, in instances where square footage is used to estimate costs, a software program was used to roughly estimate the square footage based on the floorplan depiction in Figure 3.1. All other assumptions are discussed below in the details for each option.

Option 5.A: 50/50 Split of the Sleeping Bay without Changing Rooms

The following option allows for a 50/50 split between bay areas to allow half male and half female occupancy. This option does not include a separate area for changing. This option requires the least amount of modifications and hence is the least costly. Figure B.1 is a notional depiction of the floorplan with modifications. The circled numbers correspond to the list of modifications depicted below.

Figure B.1. 50/50 Split of Sleeping Bay without Changing Rooms

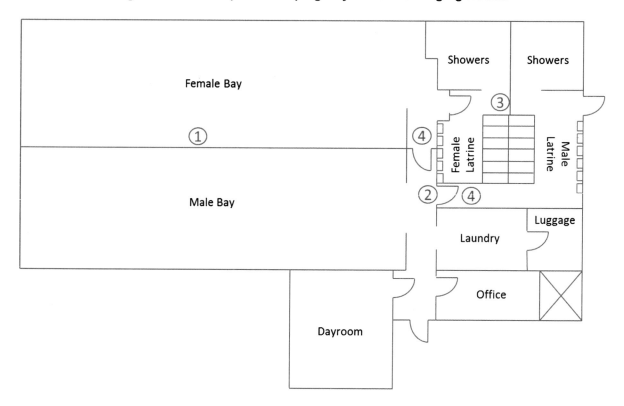

NOTE: This figure is a notional depiction of the bay area with modifications. It is not drawn to scale but is meant to provide a general idea of the modifications.

The modifications for this option include

- filling in the wall between the bays, including building the wall to the ceiling and closing off the opening on the far wall between the bays[1]
- removing a sink and creating a doorway and hall to the male latrine by adding a wall to the end of the female latrine
- extending a wall between the toilets to the showers, separating the toilets for men and women
- adding two doors, including one between the hallway by the bay and one to the entrance of the male latrine.

Potential Costs

Table B.1 summarizes the costs of the modifications listed above for Option 5.A, including specific costing assumptions.

---

[1] Currently, the wall between the bays is estimated to be 7 ft, while the ceiling height is estimated at 15 ft. This would need to be closed off to completely separate the bays.

Table B.1. Cost Summary for 50/50 Split of Sleeping Bay without Changing Rooms

Modification with Assumptions	Cost per ft²/Item[a]	Ft²/Quantity	Total Cost (2015$)
1. Wall between bays (Assumes hollow concrete block partition wall with both sides drywall finished, primed, and painted with two coats)	$16.99 per ft²	677 ft²	$11,502
2. Wall closing off end of female latrine (Assumes hollow concrete block partition wall with both sides drywall finished, primed, and painted with two coats)	$16.99 per ft²	330 ft²	$5,607
3. Wall between toilets to shower (Assumes hollow concrete block partition wall with both sides drywall finished, primed, and painted with two coats)	$16.99 per ft²	375 ft²	$6,371
4. Add two doors (Assumes single hollow fireproof metal commercial door)	$1,386 per door	Two doors	$2,772
Subtotal for Option One			$26,252
Contractor Fees (25%)			$6,563
Architecture Fees (7%)			$2,297
Subtotal Before Location Adjustment			$35,112
Total Cost for Option One with Location Adjustment Factor for San Antonio, Texas (0.84)			**$29,494**

NOTE: Costs are for modifying one bay area.
[a] All costs include material and labor.

Option 5.B: 50/50 Split of the Sleeping Bay with Changing Rooms

The following option allows for a 50/50 split between bay areas to allow half male and half female occupancy. Additionally, this option includes a separate area for changing. A changing area is a critical aspect of adopting integrated sleeping bays because it provides trainees a space to change so they are never changing in the bays. Current policy stipulates that no trainee (male or female) is allowed to be in the bay area without clothing. As an example, today, all trainees are required to sleep in their PT uniform. Creating a changing area would allow this existing policy and practice to be maintained, so this option would not require a significant change to the existing routine.

Figure B.2 is a notional depiction of the floorplan with modifications. The circled numbers correspond to the list of modifications depicted below.

Figure B.2. 50/50 Split of Sleeping Bay with Changing Rooms

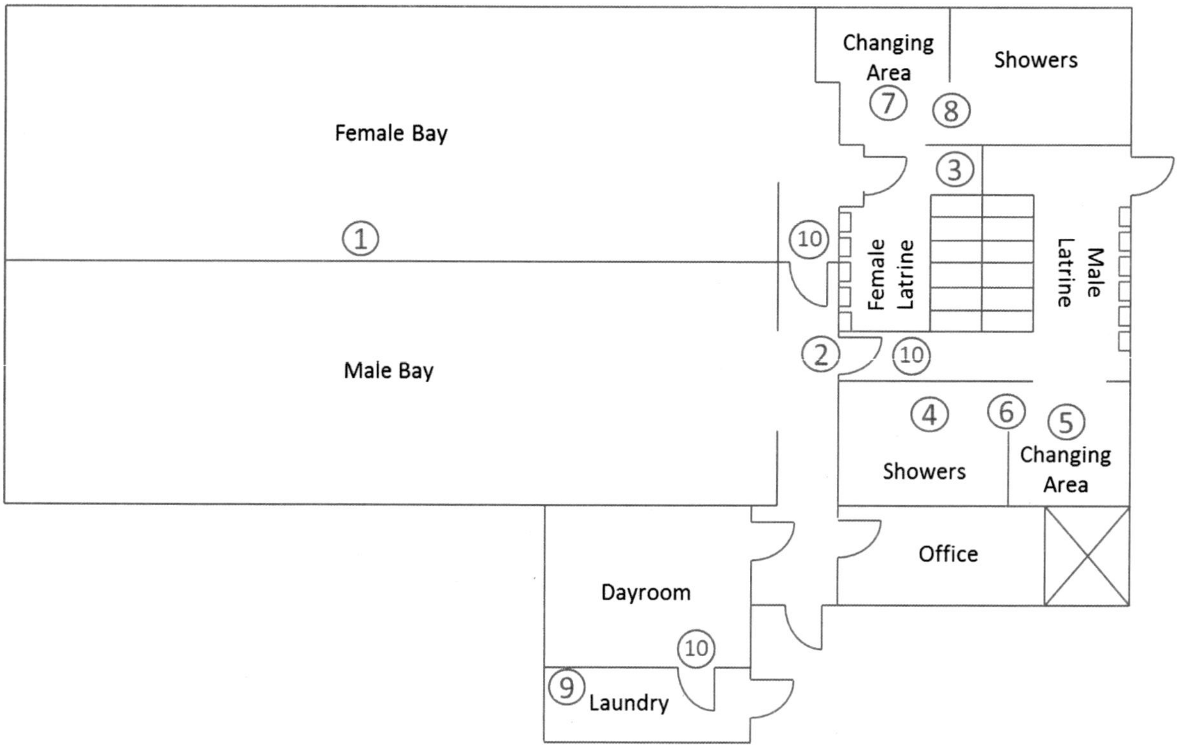

NOTE: The figure is a notional depiction of the bay area with modifications. It is not drawn to scale but is meant to provide a general idea of the modifications.

The modifications for this option include

- filling in the wall between the bays, which includes building the wall to the ceiling and closing off the opening on the far wall between the bays [2]
- removing a sink and creating a doorway and hall to the male latrine by adding a wall to the end of the female latrine
- extending a wall between the toilets to the showers separating the toilets for men and women
- converting what is currently the laundry area to a shower area for the male latrine
- converting what is currently the luggage storage area to the changing room for the male latrine
- adding a partial wall separating the shower area from the changing area in the male latrine
- converting part of the existing shower area to a changing room for the female latrine
- adding a partial wall separating the shower area from the changing area in the female latrine

---

[2] Currently, the wall between the bays is estimated to be 7 ft, while the ceiling height is estimated at 15 ft. This would need to be closed off to completely separate the bays.

- converting about a third of the dayroom to a laundry area by adding a wall, plumbing, and dryer ducts
- adding three doors including one between the hallway by the bay, one at the entrance to the male latrine, and one to the new laundry area from the dayroom.

Potential Costs

This option is more costly than the option without the changing area due to additional modifications as noted below. Table B.2 summarizes the costs of the modifications listed above for Option B, including specific costing assumptions.

Table B.2. Cost Summary for 50/50 Split of the Sleeping Bay with Changing Rooms

Modification with Assumptions	Cost per Ft²/Item[a]	Ft²/Quantity	Total Cost (2015$)
1. Wall between bays (Assumes hollow concrete block partition wall with both sides drywall finished, primed, and painted with two coats)	$16.99 per ft²	677 ft²	$11,502
2. Wall closing off end of female latrine (Assumes hollow concrete block partition wall with both sides drywall finished, primed, and painted with two coats)	$16.99 per ft²	330 ft²	$5,607
3. Wall between toilets to shower (Assumes hollow concrete block partition wall with both sides drywall finished, primed, and painted with two coats)	$16.99 per ft²	375 ft²	$6,371
4. Convert laundry area to shower area (male latrine) (Cost per item assumes group of six shower heads, thermostatic mix valves and balancing valve; assumes nine shower heads required)	$13,355 per six-shower head group	1.5 (six-shower head group=nine shower heads)	$20,033
5. Convert luggage area to changing area (male latrine) (Assumes minimal cost)	$44.59 per ft²	150 ft²	$6,689
6. Add partial wall separating shower/ changing areas (male latrine) (Assumes hollow concrete block partition wall with both sides tiled)			$0
7. Create changing room (female latrine) (Assumes minimal cost)			$0
8. Add partial wall separating shower/ changing areas (female latrine) (Assumes hollow concrete block partition wall with both sides tiled)	$44.59 per ft²	150 ft²	$6,689

9.	Add laundry room in dayroom (Assumes hollow concrete block partition wall with both sides drywall; finished, primed, and painted with two coats)	$16.99 per ft^2	435 ft^2	$7,391
10.	Add three doors (Assumes single hollow fireproof metal commercial door)	$1,386 per door	Three doors	$4,158
Subtotal for Option Two without Fees				$61,750
Contractor Fees (25%)				$15,437
Architecture Fees (7%)				$5,403
Subtotal Before Location Adjustment				$82,590
Total Cost with Location Adjustment Factor for San Antonio, Texas (0.84)				**$69,376**

NOTE: Costs are for modifying one bay area.
[a] All costs include material and labor.

Option 5.C: 75/25 Split of the Sleeping Bay with Changing Rooms

The following option allows for a 75/25 split between bay areas to allow for integrated male and female occupancy at a ratio closer to 75 percent and 25 percent. In this option, one entire bay would be assigned to men; the other bay would be split 50/50 between men and women, and an accordion wall would separate the male and female spaces.[3]

In this option, other modifications would also need to be made. For instance, the sleeping bays currently have one latrine because all the occupants of the bay are the same sex. If bays were integrated, it would require modifications to accommodate separate latrine facilities. As explained in Option 5.B, the inclusion of a changing area is crucial to integrating the sleeping bays. Therefore, this option also includes a separate area for changing.

This option is the most costly option but is very similar to Option 5.B in most ways. However, it adds an accordion wall to split half of one side of the sleeping bay. Figure B.3 is a notional depiction of the floorplan with modifications. The circled numbers correspond to the list of modifications depicted below.

---

[3] We did not include a 75/25 option without a changing room because that would be logistically difficult.

Figure B.3. 75/25 Split of Sleeping Bay with Changing Rooms

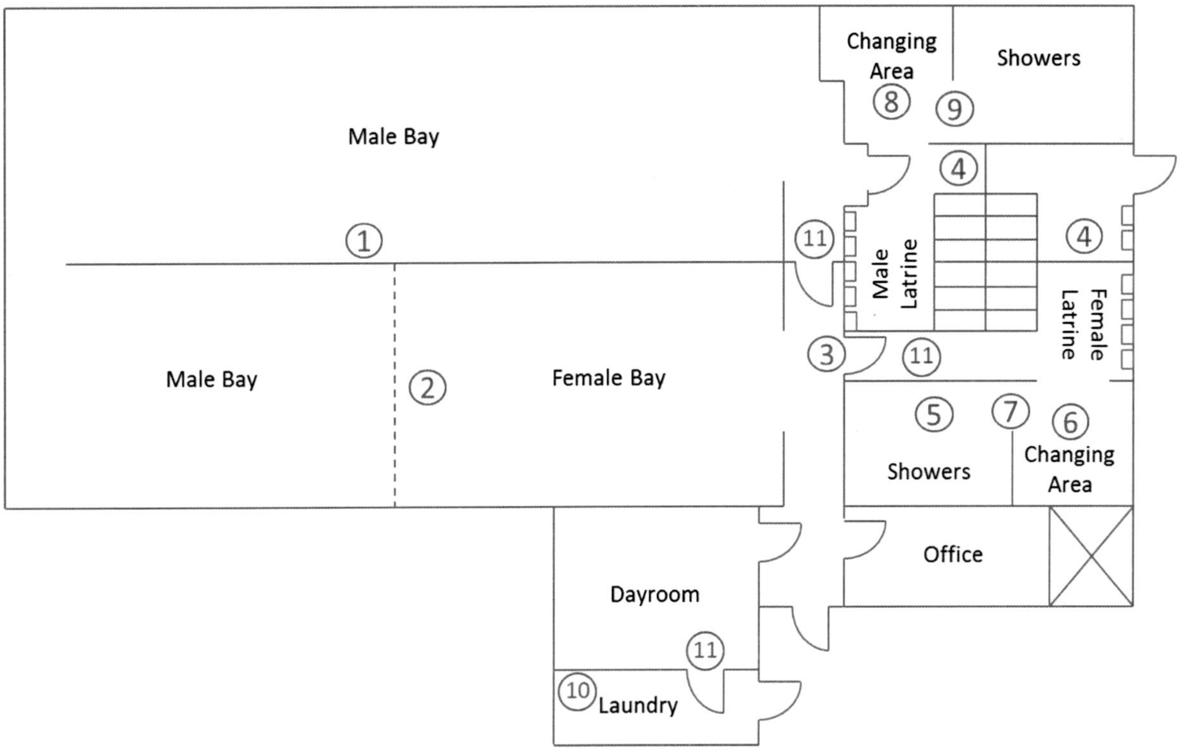

NOTE: The following figure is a notional depiction of the bay area with modifications. It is not drawn to scale but is meant to provide a general idea of the modifications.

The modifications for this option include

- filling in the current wall between the bays by building the wall to the ceiling;[4] the opening between bays will remain to allow for the larger ratio gender (presumed to be male) to pass through to their respective half of the other sleeping bay
- adding an accordion wall to split half of the one bay (the accordion wall allows flexibility in configurations)
- removing a sink and creating a doorway and hall to the male latrine by adding a wall to the end of the female latrine
- extending a wall between the toilets to the showers separating the toilets for men and women; add a wall to leave approximately one-quarter of the sinks and toilets for the female latrine and three-quarters for the male latrine.
- converting what is currently the laundry area to a shower area for the male latrine
- converting what is currently the luggage storage are to the changing room for the male latrine
- adding a partial wall separating the shower area from the changing area in the male latrine

---

[4] Currently, the wall between the bays is estimated to be 7 ft, while the ceiling height is estimated at 15 ft. This would need to be closed off to completely separate the bays.

- converting part of the existing shower area to a changing room for the female latrine
- adding a partial wall separating the shower area from the changing area in the female latrine
- converting about a third of the dayroom to a laundry area by adding a wall, plumbing, and dryer ducts
- adding three doors, including one between the hallway by the sleeping bay, one at the entrance to the female latrine, and one to the new laundry area from the dayroom.

Potential Costs

Table B.3 summarizes the costs of the modifications listed above for Option 5.C, including specific costing assumptions.

Table B.3. Cost Summary for 75/25 Split of the Sleeping Bay with Changing Rooms

Modification with Assumptions	Cost per Ft^2/Item[a]	Ft^{2}Quantity	Total Cost (2015$)
1. Wall between bays (Assumes hollow concrete block partition wall with both sides drywall finished, primed, and painted with two coats)	$16.99 per ft^2	632 ft^2	$10,738
2. Install accordion wall splitting one sleeping bay (Assumes 5 lb per sq ft vinyl covered, acoustical folding accordion partition)	$60.65 per ft^2	390 ft^2	$23,654
3. Wall closing off end of female latrine (Assumes hollow concrete block partition wall with both sides drywall finished, primed, and painted with two coats)	$16.99 per ft^2	330 ft^2	$5,607
4. Wall between toilets to shower (Assumes hollow concrete block partition wall with both sides drywall finished, primed, and painted with two coats)	$16.99 per ft^2	375 ft^2	$6,371
5. Convert laundry area to shower area (male latrine) (Cost per item assumes group of six shower heads, thermostatic mix valves and balancing valve; estimate assumes nine shower heads required)	$13,355 per six-shower head group	1.5 (six-shower head group=9 shower heads)	$20,033
6. Convert luggage area to changing area (male latrine) (Assumes minimal cost)			$0
7. Add partial wall separating shower/ changing areas (male latrine) (Assumes hollow concrete block partition wall with both sides tiled)	$44.59 per ft^2	150 ft^2	$6,689
8. Create changing room (female latrine) (Assumes minimal cost)			$0

9. Add partial wall separating shower/ changing areas (female latrine) (Assumes hollow concrete block partition wall with both sides tiled)	$44.59 per ft^2	150 ft^2	$6,689
10. Add laundry room in dayroom (Assumes hollow concrete block partition wall with both sides drywall finished, primed, and painted with two coats)	$16.99 per ft^2	435 ft^2	$7,391
11. Add three doors (Assumes single hollow fireproof metal commercial door)	$1,386 per door	Three doors	$4,158
Subtotal for Option Three without fees			$84,639
Contractor Fees (25%)			$21,160
Architecture Fees (7%)			$7,406
Subtotal Before Location Adjustment			$113,204
Total Cost for Option Three with Location Adjustment Factor for San Antonio, Texas (0.84)			**$95,091**

NOTE: Costs are for modifying one bay area.

[a] All costs include material and labor.

Appendix C: Monitoring Framework for Implementing GIT in BMT

Table C.1. Monitoring Framework for Implementation of GIT: Planning Phase (Before Implementation Begins)

DOTMLPF-P(A) Categories	Issues	Metrics	Methods
Organization	Is the USAF prepared to assess and potentially revise BMT training procedures as needed to support increased GIT at BMT?	Plan in place to periodically review and potentially revise BMT training as needed; a group of people identified as responsible for conducting this review	Qualitative review of policy and practices
	Has the USAF developed an implementation plan related to the implementation of GIT in BMT?	Implementation plan has been developed for GIT in BMT	Qualitative review of policy and practices
	Has the USAF developed the organizational culture to support increased levels of GIT in BMT?	Degree to which the USAF has developed the organizational culture to support increased levels of GIT in BMT	Survey, interview, or focus group data
Training	At what rates are men and women entering BMT?	Rates at which men and women are entering BMT	Administrative data
	What are graduation rates of male and female trainees at BMT in gender-integrated flights?	Graduation rates of male and female trainees at BMT in gender-integrated flights	Administrative data
	What are graduation rates of male and female trainees at BMT in gender-segregated flights?	Graduation rates of male and female trainees at BMT in gender-segregated flights	Administrative data
	What are retention rates of male and female trainees at BMT in gender-integrated flights?	Retention rates of male and female trainees at BMT in gender-integrated flights	Administrative data
	What are retention rates of male and female trainees at BMT in gender-segregated flights?	Retention rates of male and female trainees at BMT in gender-segregated flights	Administrative data
	What are attrition rates of male and female trainees at BMT in gender-integrated flights?	Attrition rates of male and female trainees at BMT in gender-integrated flights	Administrative data
	What are attrition rates of male and female trainees at BMT in gender-segregated flights?	Attrition rates of male and female trainees at BMT in gender-segregated flights	Administrative data
	What are the primary reasons why male trainees attrite?	Primary reasons why male trainees attrite	Administrative data; survey data
	What are the primary reasons why female trainees attrite?	Primary reasons why female trainees attrite	Administrative data; survey data

DOTMLPF-P(A) Categories	Issues	Metrics	Methods
	Do physical fitness tests in BMT differ for male and female trainees? If so, how are they different?	Ways in which physical fitness tests in BMT differ for male and female trainees	Administrative data
	What are male completion rates for physical fitness tests in BMT?	Male completion rates for physical fitness tests in BMT	Administrative data
	What are female completion rates for physical fitness test in BMT?	Female completion rates for physical fitness tests in BMT	Administrative data
	What percentage of BMT training flights are currently gender-integrated?	Percentage of BMT training flights that are currently gender-integrated	Administrative data
	What percentage of male trainees currently experience GIT during BMT?	Percentage male trainees who currently experience GIT during BMT	Administrative data; survey data
	What percentage of female trainees currently experience GIT during BMT?	Percentage female trainees who currently experience GIT during BMT	Administrative data; survey data
	Are there any BMT training activities that are not gender-integrated? If so, what are they and in what ways are they not gender-integrated?	List of BMT training activities that are not gender-integrated and ways in which they are not gender-integrated	Qualitative review of policy and practices; administrative data; survey, interview, or focus group data
	If there are any BMT training activities that are not gender-integrated, why are they not gender-integrated?	Reasons why some BMT training activities are not gender-integrated	Qualitative review of policy and practices; administrative data; survey, interview, or focus group data
	Do female trainees fall out in the morning in GIT flights or gender-segregated training flights?	Percentage of female trainees who fall out in GIT flights and percentage of female trainees who fall out in gender-segregated training flights	Qualitative review of policy and practices; administrative data
	Do male trainees fall out in the morning in GIT flights or gender-segregated training flights?	Percentage of male trainees who fall out in GIT flights and percentage of male trainees who fall out in gender-segregated training flights	Qualitative review of policy and practices; administrative data
	Is academic or technical content taught in mixed-gender classrooms? If so, what is the proportion of male to female trainees?	Proportion of academic or technical content that is taught in mixed-gender classroom; proportion of male to female trainees in classrooms	Qualitative review of policy and practices; administrative data
	Do male and female trainees sleep in separate all-male or all-female open bay sleeping areas?	Percentage of male and female trainees who sleep in separate all-male or all-female open bay sleeping areas	Qualitative review of policy and practices
	Do male and female trainees sleep in gender-integrated open bay sleeping areas?	Percentage of male and female trainees who sleep in gender-integrated open bay sleeping areas	Qualitative review of policy and practices; administrative data

98

DOTMLPF-P(A) Categories	Issues	Metrics	Methods
	Do male and female trainees sleep in gender-segregated or gender-integrated dorm buildings?	Percentage of male and female trainees who sleep in gender-segregated dorm buildings and percentage of male and female trainees who sleep in gender-integrated dorm buildings	Qualitative review of policy and practices; administrative data
	Do any formal BMT training activities take place in the sleeping bays? If so, are those training activities gender-integrated or gender-segregated?	Types and numbers of formal BMT gender-integrated training activities that take place in the sleeping bays and types and numbers of formal BMT gender-segregated training activities that take place in the sleeping bays	Qualitative review of policy and practices; administrative data
	Do MTIs sleep in the trainee sleeping bays at any time?	Whether MTIs sleep in the trainee sleeping bays at any time	Qualitative review of policy and practices
	Do MTIs sleep elsewhere in the dorm buildings at any time?	Whether MTIs sleep elsewhere in the dorm buildings at any time	Qualitative review of policy and practices
Materiel	Do data systems exist to track necessary changes to uniforms, footwear, and equipment for male and female trainees?	Data systems exist to track necessary changes to uniforms, footwear, and equipment for male and female trainees	Qualitative review of policy and practices
Leadership and Education	Has a coordinated series of training classes focused on gender issues been developed for MTIs and BMT commanders?	A coordinated series of training classes on gender issues has been developed for MTIs and BMT commanders	Qualitative review of policy and practices
	Are male trainees receiving the mentorship and support they need?	Rates at which male trainees feel they are receiving the mentorship and support they need	Survey, interview, or focus group data
	Are female trainees receiving the mentorship and support they need?	Rates at which female trainees feel they are receiving the mentorship and support they need	Survey, interview, or focus group data
	What are the primary sources of mentorship and support for male trainees?	Primary sources of mentorship and support for male trainees	Survey, interview, or focus group data
	What are the primary sources of mentorship and support for female trainees?	Primary sources of mentorship and support for female trainees	Survey, interview, or focus group data
	Which avenues of support provide the greatest assistance to male trainees?	Avenues of support that provide the greatest assistance to male trainees	Survey, interview, or focus group data
	Which avenues of support provide the greatest assistance to female trainees?	Avenues of support that provide the greatest assistance to female trainees	Survey, interview, or focus group data

DOTMLPF-P(A) Categories	Issues	Metrics	Methods
	Do mechanisms exist to assess the status of mentorship and support to male and female trainees?	Mechanisms exist to assess the status of mentorship and support to female trainees	Administrative data; survey, interview, or focus group data
	Are there mentors and advisors of both genders available to trainees?	Mentors and advisors of both genders are available to trainees	Survey, interview, or focus group data
Personnel	How many MTIs are assigned to each training flight?	Number of MTIs assigned to each training flight	Administrative data
	Are MTIs responsible for a single or multiple training flights?	Number of flights that MTIs are responsible for	Qualitative review of policy and practices
	If multiple MTIs are assigned to a training flight, are MTI teams gender-integrated?	Percentage of MTI teams that are gender-integrated	Qualitative review of policy and practices
	Do MTIs have adequate professional development opportunities?	MTIs indicate that they have adequate professional development opportunities	Qualitative review of policy and practices; survey, interview, or focus group data
	Are there plans in place to increase professional development opportunities for MTIs?	Plans are in place to increase professional development opportunities for MTIs	Qualitative review of policy and practices
Facilities	Are any facilities changes planned related to GIT? If so, what are they?	Facilities changes related to GIT	Qualitative review of policy and practices
	Do data systems exist to track changes to existing facilities and plans for modifications?	Data systems exist to track changes to existing facilities and plans for modifications	Qualitative review of policy and practices
Policy	Has the USAF developed a logic model for implementing and evaluating GIT?	The USAF has developed a logic model for implementing and evaluating GIT	Qualitative review of policy and practices
	Has the USAF developed plans for internal and external communications about GIT efforts?	The USAF has developed plans for internal and external communications about GIT efforts	Qualitative review of policy and practices
	Has the USAF developed a plan for oversight of GIT and assigned responsibility for oversight?	The USAF has developed a plan for oversight of GIT and assigned responsibility for oversight	Qualitative review of policy and practices
	Do all necessary data systems exist to collect data relevant to monitoring implementation of increased GIT in BMT?	All necessary data systems exist to collect data relevant to monitoring implementation of increased GIT in BMT	Qualitative review of policy and practices
	Do initial budget and resource allocations exist for implementing increased GIT in BMT?	Initial budget and resource allocations exist for implementing increased GIT in BMT	Qualitative review of policy and practices
	Does a plan exist to minimize instances of misconduct and complaints related to GIT?	Plan exists to minimize instances of misconduct and complaints related to GIT	Qualitative review of policy and practices

DOTMLPF-P(A) Categories	Issues	Metrics	Methods
Attitudinal	Do data systems exist to track and assess instances of misconduct along with complaints and investigations related to GIT?	Data systems exist to track and assess instances of misconduct along with complaints and investigations related to GIT	Qualitative review of policy and practices
	Do procedures exist to address and investigate instances of misconduct and complaints related to GIT?	Procedures exist to address and investigate instances of misconduct and complaints related to GIT	Qualitative review of policy and practices
	Are mechanisms in place for male and female trainees to seek redress outside the chain of command for GIT-related issues?	Mechanisms in place for male and female trainees to seek redress outside the chain of command for GIT-related issues	Qualitative review of policy and practices
	How are complaints related to GIT expected to be addressed?	Description of how complaints related to GIT are expected to be addressed	Qualitative review of policy and practices
	Are there support services available for male and female trainees making complaints related to GIT issues?	Support services are available for male and female trainees making complaints related to GIT issues	Qualitative review of policy and practices; administrative data
	What is the level of morale among male trainees?	Level of morale among male trainees	Survey, interview, or focus group data
	What is the level of morale among female trainees?	Level of morale among female trainees	Survey, interview, or focus group data
	What is the level of cohesion among male trainees?	Level of cohesion among male trainees	Survey, interview, or focus group data
	What is the level of cohesion among female trainees?	Level of cohesion among female trainees	Survey, interview, or focus group data

Table C.2. Monitoring Framework for Implementation of GIT: Implementation Phase (After Implementation Begins)

DOTMLPF-P(A) Categories	Issues	Metrics	Methods
Organization	Is the USAF assessing and potentially revising BMT training procedures as needed to support increased GIT in BMT?	Periodic reviews of GIT are occurring	Qualitative review of policy and practices
	Is the USAF implementation plan for GIT in BMT being followed?	Implementation plan for GIT in BMT is being followed	Qualitative review of policy and practices
	Has the USAF developed the organizational culture to support increased levels of GIT in BMT?	Degree to which the USAF has developed the organizational culture to support increased levels of GIT in BMT	Survey, interview or focus group data
Training	At what rates are men and women entering BMT?	Rates at which men and women are entering BMT	Administrative data
	What are graduation rates of male trainees at BMT in gender-integrated flights?	Graduation rates of male trainees at BMT in gender-integrated flights	Administrative data
	What are graduation rates of female trainees at BMT in gender-segregated flights?	Graduation rates of female trainees at BMT in gender-segregated flights	Administrative data
	What are retention rates of male trainees at BMT in gender-integrated flights?	Retention rates of male trainees at BMT in gender-integrated flights	Administrative data
	What are retention rates of female trainees at BMT in gender-segregated flights?	Retention rates of female trainees at BMT in gender-segregated flights	Administrative data
	What are attrition rates of male trainees at BMT in gender-integrated flights?	Attrition rates of male trainees at BMT in gender-integrated flights	Administrative data
	What are attrition rates of female trainees at BMT in gender-segregated flights?	Attrition rates of female trainees at BMT in gender-segregated flights	Administrative data
	What are the primary reasons why male trainees attrite?	Primary reasons why male trainees attrite	Administrative data; survey data
	What are the primary reasons why female trainees attrite?	Primary reasons why female trainees attrite	Administrative data; survey data
	Do physical fitness tests in BMT differ for male and female trainees? If so, how are they different?	Ways in which physical fitness tests in BMT differ for male and female trainees	Administrative data
	What are male completion rates for physical fitness tests in BMT?	Male completion rates for physical fitness tests in BMT	Administrative data
	What are female completion rates for physical fitness tests in BMT?	Female completion rates for physical fitness tests in BMT	Administrative data
	What percentage of BMT training flights are currently gender-integrated?	Percentage of BMT training flights that are currently gender-integrated	Administrative data

102

DOTMLPF-P(A) Categories	Issues	Metrics	Methods
	What percentage of male trainees currently experience GIT during BMT?	Percentage male of trainees who currently experience GIT during BMT	Administrative data
	What percentage of female trainees currently experience GIT during BMT?	Percentage of female trainees who currently experience GIT during BMT	Administrative data; survey data
	Are there any BMT training activities that are not gender-integrated? If so, what are they and in what ways are they not gender-integrated?	List of BMT training activities that are not gender-integrated and ways in which they are not gender-integrated	Qualitative review of policy and practices; administrative data; survey, interview, or focus group data
	If there are any BMT training activities that are not gender-integrated, why are they not gender-integrated?	Training activities that are not gender-integrated and why are they not gender-integrated	Qualitative review of policy and practices
	Do male trainees fall out in the morning in GIT flights or gender-segregated training flights?	Percentage of male trainees that fall out in GIT flights or gender-segregated training flights	Qualitative review of policy and practices
	Do female trainees fall out in the morning in GIT flights or gender-segregated training flights?	Percentage of female trainees that fall out in GIT flights or gender-segregated training flights	Qualitative review of policy and practices
	Is academic or technical content taught in mixed-gender classrooms? If so, what is the proportion of male to female trainees?	Proportion of academic or technical content that is taught in mixed-gender classroom; proportion of male to female trainees in classrooms	Qualitative review of policy and practices; administrative data
	Do male and female trainees sleep in separate all-male or all-female open bay sleeping areas?	Percentage of male and female trainees that sleep in separate all-male or all-female open bay sleeping areas	Qualitative review of policy and practices
	Do male and female trainees sleep in gender-integrated open bay sleeping areas?	Percentage of male and female trainees that sleep in gender-integrated open bay sleeping areas	Qualitative review of policy and practices; administrative data
	Do any formal BMT training activities take place in the sleeping bays? If so, are those training activities gender-integrated or gender-segregated?	Formal BMT training activities that take place in the sleeping bays and whether they are gender-integrated or gender-segregated	Qualitative review of policy and practices; administrative data
	Do MTIs sleep in the trainee sleeping bays at any time?	Whether MTIs sleep in the trainee sleeping bays at any time	Qualitative review of policy and practices
	Do MTIs sleep elsewhere in the dorm buildings at any time?	Whether MTIs sleep elsewhere in the dorm buildings at any time	Qualitative review of policy and practices
Materiel	Are changes to uniforms, footwear, and equipment for male and female trainees being tracked?	Changes to uniforms, footwear, and equipment for male and female trainees are being tracked	Review of USAF policy

DOTMLPF-P(A) Categories	Issues	Metrics	Methods
	Have new materiel issues arisen since the start of increased GIT that need to be addressed?	Any new materiel issues have been identified	Surveys of male and female users
Leadership and Education	Has a coordinated series of training classes focused on gender issues been implemented for MTIs and BMT commanders?	A coordinated series of training classes on gender issues has been implemented for MTIs and BMT commanders	Review of USAF policy
	Are male trainees receiving the mentorship and support they need?	Rates at which male trainees feel they are receiving the mentorship and support they need	Survey, interview, or focus group data
	Are female trainees receiving the mentorship and support they need?	Rates at which female trainees feel they are receiving the mentorship and support they need	Survey, interview, or focus group data
	What are the primary sources of mentorship and support for male trainees?	Primary sources of mentorship and support for male trainees	Survey, interview, or focus group data
	What are the primary sources of mentorship and support for female trainees?	Primary sources of mentorship and support for female trainees	Survey, interview, or focus group data
	Do male trainees feel that they receive sufficient support?	Rates at which male trainees feel they receive sufficient support	Survey, interview, or focus group data
	Do female trainees feel that they receive sufficient support?	Rates at which female trainees feel they receive sufficient support	Survey, interview, or focus group data
	Which avenues of support provide the greatest assistance to male trainees?	Avenues of support that provide the greatest assistance to male trainees	Survey, interview, or focus group data
	Which avenues of support provide the greatest assistance to female trainees?	Avenues of support that provide the greatest assistance to female trainees	Survey, interview, or focus group data
	Do mechanisms exist to assess the status of mentorship and support to male and female trainees?	Mechanisms exist to assess the status of mentorship and support to female trainees	Administrative data; survey, interview, or focus group data
	Are there mentors and advisors of both genders available to trainees?	Mentors and advisors of both genders are available to trainees	Survey, interview, or focus group data
Personnel	How many MTIs are assigned to each training flight?	Number of MTIs assigned to each training flight	Administrative data
	Are MTIs responsible for a single or multiple training flights?	Number of flights that MTIs are responsible for	Qualitative review of policy and practices
	If multiple MTIs are assigned to a training flight, are MTI teams gender-integrated?	Percentage of MTI teams that are gender-integrated	Qualitative review of policy and practices
	Do MTIs have adequate professional development opportunities?	MTIs indicate that they have adequate professional development opportunities	Qualitative review of policy and practices; survey, interview, or focus group data

DOTMLPF-P(A) Categories	Issues	Metrics	Methods
	Have plans to increase professional development opportunities for MTIs been implemented?	Plans to increase professional development opportunities for MTIs have been implemented	Qualitative review of policy and practices
Facilities	Have any facilities changes related to GIT been made? If so, what are they?	Facilities changes related to GIT that have been made	Qualitative review of policy and practices
	Are any new facilities changes related to GIT planned?	Facilities changes related to GIT that are planned	Qualitative review of policy and practices
	Are changes to existing facilities and plans for modifications being tracked?	Changes to existing facilities and plans for modifications are being tracked	Qualitative review of policy and practices
Policy	Has the USAF developed and utilized a logic model for implementing and evaluating GIT?	The USAF has developed and utilized a logic model for implementing and evaluating GIT	Qualitative review of policy and practices
	Has the USAF implemented plans for internal and external communications about GIT efforts?	The USAF has implemented plans for internal and external communications about GIT efforts	Qualitative review of policy and practices
	Has the USAF implemented a plan for oversight of GIT and assigned responsibility for oversight?	The USAF has implemented a plan for oversight of GIT and assigned responsibility for oversight	Qualitative review of policy and practices
	Is all necessary data required to monitor implementation of increased GIT in BMT being collected?	All necessary data required to monitor implementation of increased GIT in BMT is being collected	Qualitative review of policy and practices
	Do continuing budget and resource allocations exist for implementing increased GIT in BMT?	Continuing budget and resource allocations exist for implementing increased GIT in BMT	Qualitative review of policy and practices
	Has a plan to minimize instances of misconduct and complaints related to GIT been implemented?	Plan to minimize instances of misconduct and complaints related to GIT has been implemented	Qualitative review of policy and practices
	Are policies regarding GIT being implemented consistently across training flights and squadrons?	Policies regarding GIT are being implemented consistently across training flights and squadrons	Qualitative review of policy and practices; survey, interview, and focus group data
Attitudinal	Are instances of misconduct along with complaints and investigations related to GIT being tracked?	Instances of misconduct along with complaints and investigations related to GIT are being tracked	Qualitative review of policy and practices
	Do procedures exist to address and investigate instances of misconduct and complaints related to GIT?	Procedures exist to address and investigate instances of misconduct and complaints related to GIT	Qualitative review of policy and practices

DOTMLPF-P(A) Categories	Issues	Metrics	Methods
	Are mechanisms in place for male and female trainees to seek redress outside the chain of command for GIT-related issues?	Mechanisms in place for male and female trainees to seek redress outside the chain of command for GIT-related issues	Qualitative review of policy and practices
	Are stated procedures for addressing and investigating misconduct and complaints related to GIT being followed?	Degree to which stated procedures for addressing and investigating misconduct and complaints related to GIT are being followed	Qualitative review of policy and practices; administrative data
	How are complaints related to GIT currently being addressed?	Description of how complaints related to GIT are currently being addressed	Qualitative review of policy and practices
	Are there support services available for male and female trainees making complaints related to GIT?	Support services are available for male and female trainees making complaints related to GIT	Qualitative review of policy and practices; administrative data
	Are the support services available for male trainees making GIT-related complaints adequate?	Support services are adequate for male trainees making GIT-related complaints	Survey, interview or focus group data
	Are the support services available for female trainees making GIT-related complaints adequate?	Support services are adequate for female trainees making GIT-related complaints	Survey, interview or focus group data
	How do trends in instances of misconduct, investigations, and complaints related to GIT in BMT compare over time?	Analysis of trends over time of instances of misconduct and complaints related to GIT in BMT	Survey data; administrative data
	What challenges or obstacles have male trainees experienced since the start of GIT?	Challenges or obstacles that male trainees have experienced since the start of GIT	Survey, interview, or focus group data
	What challenges or obstacles have female trainees experienced since the start of GIT?	Challenges or obstacles that female trainees have experienced since the start of GIT	Survey, interview, or focus group data
	What is the level of morale among male trainees?	Level of morale among male trainees	Survey, interview, or focus group data
	What is the level of morale among female trainees?	Level of morale among female trainees	Survey, interview, or focus group data
	Have levels of morale among male trainees changed over time?	Level of morale among male trainees over time	Survey, interview, or focus group data
	Have levels of morale among female trainees changed over time?	Level of morale among female trainees over time	Survey, interview, or focus group data
	What is the level of cohesion among male trainees?	Level of cohesion among male trainees	Survey, interview, or focus group data
	What is the level of cohesion among male trainees?	Level of cohesion among female trainees	Survey, interview, or focus group data
	Have levels of cohesion among male trainees changed over time?	Level of cohesion among male trainees over time	Survey, interview, or focus group data

DOTMLPF-P(A) Categories	Issues	Metrics	Methods
	Have levels of cohesion among female trainees changed over time?	Level of cohesion among female trainees over time	Survey, interview, or focus group data

107

Appendix D: RAND Flight Optimization Model

As part of this study, RAND developed a flight optimization model to help the USAF determine the optimal proportion of men and women across flights given the size of the incoming class. In Step One, the user inputs the number of incoming male and female trainees. In Step Two, the tool identifies how many male and female sleeping bays are needed. In Step Three, the tool identifies how many flights of different sizes are needed to most optimally assign men and women to flights, depending on the GIT option chosen.

Figure D.1. Step One: User Inputs Number of Incoming Trainees to Identify How Many Flights Are Needed

Incoming Class of Male Trainees	Incoming Class of Female Trainees	Total Incoming Class?	Total Flights Needed?
525	175	700	16

Figure D.2. Step Two: Tool Identifies Number of Male and Female Dorms Needed for Incoming Class

	Incoming Class of Male Trainees	Incoming Class of Female Trainees	Total Number of Male Dorms Needed	Total Number of Female Dorms Needed	Total Number of Dorms Needed
Total Trainees	525	175	9	3	12
Unassigned people	110	25			

	Gender of Dorm (1 = Male)	Gender of Dorm (1 = Female)	# of Trainees in Dorm	Number of these Dorms	Number of these Male Dorms	Number of these Female Dorms
	1	0	42	5	5	0
	1	0	43	0	0	0
	1	0	44	0	0	0
	1	0	45	0	0	0
	1	0	46	0	0	0
	1	0	47	0	0	0
	1	0	48	0	0	0
	1	0	49	1	1	0
	1	0	50	0	0	0
	1	0	51	0	0	0
	1	0	52	3	3	0
	0	1	42	0	0	0
	0	1	43	0	0	0
	0	1	44	0	0	0
	0	1	45	0	0	0
	0	1	46	0	0	0
	0	1	47	0	0	0
	0	1	48	0	0	0
	0	1	49	0	0	0
	0	1	50	3	0	3
	0	1	51	0	0	0
	0	1	52	0	0	0

Figure D.3. Step Three: Tool Assigns Incoming Class to Integrated Flights Based on Various GIT Models and Calculates Female Attrition (75/25 Model)

Bay Sizes	Gender	Number of Bays	Bay	Bay Gender	Bay Size	Integrated Training Flights	Males in Integrated Training Flight	Females in Integrated Training Flight	Total Trainees in Integrated Training Flight	Female Proportion Within Training Flight	Female Trainees Remaining After Average Attrition	Female Trainees Remaining After High Attrition	Female Trainees Remaining After Extremely High Attrition
52	Male	0	1	Male	49	1	37	12	49	22.45%	10	10	10
51	Male	0	2	Male	49	2	37	12	49	22.45%	10	10	10
50	Male	0	3	Male	49	3	37	12	49	22.45%	10	10	10
49	Male	3	4	Male	42	4	32	12	44	25.00%	10	10	10
48	Male	0	5	Male	42	5	32	12	44	25.00%	10	10	10
47	Male	0	6	Male	42	6	32	12	44	25.00%	10	10	10
46	Male	0	7	Male	42	7	32	11	43	25.58%	10	9	9
45	Male	0	8	Male	42	8	32	11	43	25.58%	10	9	9
44	Male	0	9	Male	42	9	32	11	43	25.58%	10	9	9
43	Male	0	10	Male	42	10	32	10	42	23.81%	9	8	8
42	Male	9	11	Male	42	11	32	10	42	23.81%	9	8	8
52	Female	0	12	Male	42	12	32	10	42	23.81%	9	8	8
51	Female	0	13	Female	45	13	32	10	42	23.81%	9	8	8
50	Female	0	14	Female	44	14	32	10	42	23.81%	9	8	8
49	Female	0	15	Female	44	15	31	10	41	24.39%	9	8	8
48	Female	0	16	Female	42	16	31	10	41	24.39%	9	8	8
47	Female	0	17			17			0	N/A	N/A	N/A	N/A
46	Female	0	18			18			0	N/A	N/A	N/A	N/A
45	Female	1	19			19			0	N/A	N/A	N/A	N/A
44	Female	2	20			20			0	N/A	N/A	N/A	N/A
43	Female	0											
42	Female	1											

Figure D.3. Step Three: Tool Assigns Incoming Class to Integrated Flights Based on Various GIT Models and Calculates Female Attrition (Equal Proportion of Women Across All Flights)

Bay	Bay Gender	Bay Size	Integrated Training Flights	Males in Integrated Training Flight	Females in Integrated Training Flight	Total Trainees in Integrated Training Flight	Female Proportion within Flight	Female Trainees Remaining After Average Attrition	Female Trainees Remaining After High Attrition	Female Trainees Remaining After Extremely High Attrition
1	Male	50	1	34	13	47	28%	11	11	10
2	Male	49	2	34	13	47	28%	11	11	10
3	Male	49	3	34	13	47	28%	11	11	10
4	Male	42	4	34	13	47	28%	11	11	10
5	Male	42	5	33	13	46	28%	11	11	10
6	Male	42	6	33	13	46	28%	11	11	10
7	Male	42	7	33	12	45	27%	10	10	10
8	Male	42	8	33	12	45	27%	10	10	10
9	Male	42	9	33	12	45	27%	10	10	10
10	Female	50	10	33	12	45	27%	10	10	10
11	Female	50	11	33	12	45	27%	10	10	10
12	Female	50	12	33	12	45	27%	10	10	10
13			13	0	0	0		0	0	0
14			14	0	0	0		0	0	0
15			15	0	0	0		0	0	0
16			16	0	0	0		0	0	0
17			17	0	0	0		0	0	0
18			18	0	0	0		0	0	0
19			19	0	0	0		0	0	0
20			20	0	0	0		0	0	0

References

American Association of University Women Educational Foundation, *Separated by Sex*, Washington, D.C., 1998.

Beal, Daniel J., Robin R. Cohen, Michael J. Burke, and Christy L. McLendon, "Cohesion and Performance in Groups: A Meta-Analytic Clarification of Construct Relations," *Journal of Applied Psychology,* Vol. 88, No. 6, 2003, pp. 989–1004.

Beckhard, R., and R. Harris, *Organizational Transitions: Managing Complex Change*, 2nd ed., Reading, Mass.: Addison-Wesley, 1987.

Beckwith, Karen, and Kimberly Cowell-Meyers, "Sheer Numbers: Critical Representation Thresholds and Women's Political Representation," *Perspectives on Politics*, Vol. 5, No. 3, September 2007, pp. 553–565.

Bijur, Polly E., M. Horodyski, W. Egergon, M. Kurzon, S. Lifrak, and S. Friedman, "Comparison of Injuries During Cadet Basic Training by Gender," *Archives of Pediatrics and Adolescent Medicine*, Vol. 151, No. 5, 1997, pp. 456–461.

Blair Commission—*see* U.S. Congressional Commission on Military Training and Gender-Related Issues.

Boldry, Jennifer, Wendy Wood, and Deborah A. Kashy, "Gender Stereotypes and the Evaluation of Men and Women In Military Training," *Journal of Social Issues*, Vol. 57, No. 4, 2001, pp. 689-705.

Bowman, Tom, "Congress Compromises on Mixed-Sex Military Training: Plan Would House Men, Women in Separate Barracks During Training," *Baltimore Sun*, September 26, 1998.

Brafman, Ori, and Rod A. Beckstrom, *The Starfish and the Spider: The Unstoppable Power of Leaderless Organizations*, New York: Penguin, 2006.

Broome, Lissa, John Conley, and Kimberly Krawiec, "Does Critical Mass Matter? Views from the Boardroom," *Seattle University Law Review*, Vol. 34, 2011, pp. 1049–1080.

Caiazza, Amy, "Does Women's Representation in Elected Office Lead to Women-Friendly Policy? Analysis of State-Level Data," *Women and Politics*, Vol. 26, No. 1, 2004, pp. 35–70.

Castaño, N., T. Watts, and A. G. Tekleab, "A Reexamination of the Cohesion–Performance Relationship Meta-Analyses: A Comprehensive Approach," *Group Dynamics: Theory, Research, And Practice*, Vol. 17, No. 4, 2013, pp. 207–231.

Chaney, Paul, "Critical Mass, Deliberation and the Substantive Representation of Women: Evidence from the UK's Devolution Programme," *Political Studies*, Vol. 54, No. 4, December 2006, pp. 691–714.

Chapman, Anne W., "Mixed Gender Basic Training: the United States Army Experience, 1973–2004," Training and Doctrine Command, Fort Eustis, Virginia, 2008.

Childs, Sarah, and Mona Lena Krook, "Critical Mass Theory and Women's Political Representation," *Political Studies*, Vol. 56, No. 3, 2008, pp. 725–736.

Childs, Sarah, Paul Webb, and Sally Marthaler, "Constituting and Substantively Representing Women: Applying New Approaches to a UK Case Study," *Politics and Gender*, Vol. 6, No. 2, June 2010, pp. 199–223.

"Cohen Rejects Segregating Trainees by Sex at Camp," *New York Times*, March 17, 1998.

Costa, Luis Almeida, Joao Amaro de Matos, and Miguel Pina E. Cunha, "The Manager as Change Agent: Communication Channels, Timing of Information and Attitude Change," *International Studies of Management and Organization,* Vol. 33, No. 4, Winter 2003, pp. 65–93.

Cummings, Thomas, and Christopher G Worley, *Organization Development and Change*, 5th edition, St. Paul, Minn.: West Publishing Company, 1993.

Datnow, A., and L. Hubbard, eds., *Gender in Policy and Practice: Perspectives on Single-Sex and Coeducational Schooling,* New York: Routledge, 2002.

Davis, Kristen D., "Organizational Environment and Turnover: Understanding Women's Exit from the Canadian Forces," McGill University, July 2014.

DeFleur, L. B., F. Wood, D. Harris, D. Gillman, and W. Marshak, *Four Years of Sex Integration at the United States Air Force Academy: Problems and Issues* (Tech. Rep. No. 85–10), Colorado Springs: U.S. Air Force Academy Department of Behavioral Sciences and Leadership, 1985.

Devilbiss, M. C., *Women and Military Service*, Maxwell Air Force Base, Ala.: Air University Press, 1990.

deLeon, Peter, "The Stages Approach to the Policy Process: What Has It Done? Where Is It Going?" *Theories of the Policy Process*, ed. Paul A. Sabatier, Boulder, Colo.: Westview Press, 1999, pp. 19–34.

Dooley, Susan G., "Female Recruits and the United States Marine Corps: The Transformation Process," dissertation, Monterey, Calif.: Naval Postgraduate School, March 1998.

Dreachslin, J. L., P. L. Hunt, and E. Sprainer, "Workforce Diversity: Implications for the Effectiveness of Health Care Delivery Teams," *Social Science* and *Medicine*, Vol. 50, 2000, pp. 1403–1414.

Durning, K. P., "Women at the Naval Academy: An Attitude Survey," *Armed Forces and Society*, Vol. 4, 1978, pp. 569–588.

Eberhart, Ralph E., statement before the Subcommittee on Military Personnel, Committee on National Security, House of Representatives, March 17, 1998.

Egnell, R., P. Hojem, and H. Berts, *Implementing a Gender Perspective in Military Organisations and Operations: The Swedish Armed Forces Model*, Department of Peace and Conflict Research, Uppsala University, 2012.

Evans, C. R., and K. L. Dion, "Group Cohesion and Performance: A Meta-Analysis," *Small Group Research*, Vol. 43, No. 6, 2012, pp. 690–701.

Federal Advisory Committee on Gender-Integrated Training and Related Issues, "Report of the Federal Advisory Committee on Gender-Integrated Training and Related Issues to the Secretary of Defense," Washington, D.C., December 16, 1997.

Fernandez, Sergio, and Hal G. Rainey, "Managing Successful Organizational Change in the Public Sector," *Public Administration Review*, March/April 2006, pp. 168–176.

Greed, Clara, "Women in the Construction Professions: Achieving Critical Mass," *Gender, Work, and Organization*, Vol. 7, No. 3, July 2000, pp. 181–196.

Grey, Sandra, "Women and Parliamentary Politics: Does Size Matter? Critical Mass and Women MPs in the New Zealand House of Representatives," paper written for the 51st Political Studies Association Conference in Manchester, United Kingdom, April 10–12, 2001.

Hagedorn, Linda, Winny Chi, Rita Cepeda, and Melissa McLain, "An Investigation of Critical Mass: The Role of Latino Representation in the Success of Urban Community College Students," *Research in Higher Education*, Vol. 48, No. 1, February 2007, pp. 73–91.

Halpern, D. F., L. Eliot, R. S. Bigler, R. A. Fabes, L. D. Hanish, J. Hyde and C. L. Martin, "The Pseudoscience of Single-Sex Schooling," *Science*, Vol. 333, No. 6050, 2011, pp. 1706–1707.

Harrell, Margaret C., and Laura L. Miller, *New Opportunities for Military Women: Effects Upon Readiness, Cohesion, and Morale*, Santa Monica, Calif.: RAND Corporation, 1997.

Holt, Daniel T., Achilles A. Armenakis, Hubert S. Field, and Stanley G. Harris, "Readiness for Organizational Change: The Systemic Development of a Scale," *Journal of Applied Behavioral Science*, Vol. 43, 2007, pp. 232–255.

Hogg, M. A., and D. J. Terry, "Social Identity and Self-Categorization Processes in Organizational Contexts," *Academy of Management Review,* Vol. 25, 2000, pp. 121–140.

Holm, Jeanne, *Women in the Military: An Unfinished Revolution*, Novato: Presidio Press, 1982.

Hjern, Benny, and David Porter, "Implementation Structures: A New Unit of Administrative Analysis," *Organization Studies*, Vol. 2, No. 1, 1981, pp. 211–227.

Jehn, K. A., G. B. Northcraft, and M. A. Neale, "Why Differences Make a Difference: A Field Study of Diversity, Conflict, and Performance in Workgroups, *Administrative Science Quarterly,* Vol. 44, 1999, pp. 741–763.

Joecks, Jasmin, Kerstin Pull, and Karin Vetter, "Gender Diversity in the Boardroom and Firm Performance: What Exactly Constitutes a 'Critical Mass,'" *Journal of Business Ethics*, Vol. 118, No. 1, November 2013, pp. 61–72.

Johnson, Charles, "The Study of Military Recruit Attitudes Conducive to Unit Cohesion and Survey of Military Leader Opinions on Recruit Training and Gender-Related Issues," in U.S. Congressional Commission on Military Training and Gender-Related Issues, *Congressional Commission on Military Training and Gender-Related Issues*, Vol. 3, Washington, D.C.: U.S. Government Printing Office, July 1999.

Jones, Oswald, "Developing Absorptive Capacity in Mature Organizations: The Change Agent's Role," *Management Learning*, Vol. 37, 2006, pp. 355–376.

Kanter, Rosabeth, "Some Effects of Proportions on Group Life: Skewed Sex Ratios and Responses to Token Women," *American Journal of Sociology*, Vol. 82, No. 5, March 1977, pp. 965–990.

Konrad, Alison, Vicki Kramer, and Sumru Erkut, "Critical Mass: The Impact of Three or More Women on Corporate Boards," *Organizational Dynamics*, Vol. 37, No. 2, April 2008, pp. 145–164.

Kotter, John P., *A Force for Change: How Leadership Differs From Management,* New York: Free Press, 1990.

Lambright, W. Henry, "Leadership and Change at NASA: Sean O'Keefe as Administrator," *Public Administration Review,* March/April 2008, pp. 230–240.

Laurence, Janice, Mareena Wright, Carol Keys, and Pamela Giambo, "Focus Group Research," in U.S. Congressional Commission on Military Training and Gender-Related Issues, *Congressional Commission on Military Training and Gender-Related Issues*, Vol. 4, Washington, D.C.: U.S. Government Printing Office, July 1999.

Lipsky, Michael, *Street-Level Bureaucracy: Dilemmas of Individuals in Public Services*, New York: Russell Sage, 1980.

Lee, V. E., and A. S. Bryk, "Effects of Single-Sex Secondary Schools on Student Achievement and Attitudes," *Journal of Educational Psychology*, Vol. 78, No. 5, 1986, pp. 381–395.

LePore, P., and J. R. Warren, "A Comparison of Single-Sex and Coeducational Catholic Secondary Schooling: Evidence from the National Educational Longitudinal Study of 1988," *American Educational Research Journal,* Vol. 34, 1997, pp. 485–511.

Lord, Charles G., and Delia S. Saenz, "Memory Deficits and Memory Surfeits: Differential Cognitive Consequences of Tokenism for Tokens and Observers," *Journal of Personality and Social Psychology*, Vol. 49, No. 4, October 1985, pp. 918–926.

Mael, F. A., A. Alonso, D. Gibson, K. Rogers, and M. Smith, *Single-Sex Versus Coeducational Schooling: A Systematic Review,* Washington, D.C.: U.S. Department of Education, Office of Planning, Evaluation and Policy Department, Policy and Program Studies Service, 2005.

Marsh, H. W., "Effects of Attending Single-Sex and Coeducational High Schools on Achievement, Attitudes, Behaviors, and Sex Differences," *Journal of Educational Psychology,* Vol. 81, 1989, pp. 70–85.

Martin, Patricia, Dianne Harrison, and Diana Dinitto, "Advancement for Women in Hierarchical Organizations: A Multilevel Analysis of Problems and Prospects," *Journal of Applied Behavior Science*, Vol. 19, No. 1, March 1983, pp. 19–33.

Mathieu, J. E., M. R. Kukenberger, L. D'Innocenzo, and G. Reilly, "Modeling Reciprocal Team Cohesion–Performance Relationships, as Impacted by Shared Leadership and Members' Competence," *Journal Of Applied Psychology*, Vol. 100, No. 3, 2015, pp. 713–734.

Marx, David M., and Jasmin S. Roman, "Female Role Models: Protecting Women's Math Test Performance," *Personality and Social Psychology Bulletin,* Vol. 28, No. 9, September 2002, pp. 1183–1193.

Mechanic, David, "Sources of Power of Lower Participants in Complex Organizations," *Administrative Science Quarterly*, Vol. 7, No. 3, 1962, pp. 349–364.

Moon, Michael, "Bottom-Up Instigated Organizational Change Through Constructionist Conversation," *Journal of Knowledge Management Practice*, Vol. 9, No. 4, 2008.

Mottern, Jacqueline A., David A. Foster, Elizabeth J. Brady, and Joanne Marshall-Mies, "The 1995 Gender Integration of Basic Combat Training Study," Study Report 97-01, Alexandria, Va.: United States Army Research Institute for the Behavioral and Social Sciences, 1997.

Mullen, Brian, and Carolyn Copper, "The Relation Between Group Cohesiveness and Performance: An Integration," *Psychological Bulletin,* Vol. 115, No. 2, 1994, pp. 210–227.

Myers, Meghann, "A Progressive Navy Secretary's Clash with Marines Over Jobs for Women," *Navy Times*, January 19, 2016.

Novotney, Amy, "Coed Versus Single-Sex Ed," *Monitor on Psychology*, Vol. 42, No. 2, February 2011.

Office of the Under Secretary of Defense, "FY 2016 Department of Defense (DoD) Military Personnel Composite Standard Pay and Reimbursement Rates," Memorandum for Deputy Assistant Secretary of the Air Force (Financial Management and Comptroller), Washington, D.C., March 9, 2015.

O'Reilly, C. A., D. F. Caldwell, and W. P. Barnett, "Work Group Demography, Social Integration, and Turnover," *Administrative Science Quarterly,* Vol. 34, 1989, pp. 21–37.

Oliver, Laurel W., Joan Harman, Elizabeth Hoover, Stephanie M. Hayes, and Nancy A. Pandhi, "A Quantitative Integration of the Military Cohesion Literature," *Military Psychology,* Vol. 11, No. 1, 1999, pp. 57–83.

Park, Hyunjoon, Jere R. Behrman, and Jaesun Choi, "Causal Effects of Single-Sex Schools on College Entrance Exams and College Attendance: Random Assignment in Seoul High Schools," *Demography*, Vol. 50, 2013, pp. 447–469.

Pascale, Richard T., and Jerry Sternin, "Your Company's Secret Change Agents," *Harvard Business Review*, Vol. 83, No. 5, May 2005.

Pazy, Asya, and Israela Oron, "Sex Proportion and Performance Evaluation Among High-Ranking Military Officers," *Journal of Organizational Behavior,* Vol. 22, No. 6, September 2001, pp. 689–702.

Pelled, L. H., K. M. Eisenhardt, and K. R. Xin, "Exploring the Black Box: An Analysis of Work Group Diversity, Conflict, and Performance," *Administrative Science Quarterly,* Vol. 44, 1999, pp. 1–28.

Perkins, Derrick, "Mabus: One in Four Marines Should Be Women," *Marine Corps Times*, May 25, 2015.

Poggione, Sarah, "Exploring Gender Differences in State Legislators' Policy Preferences," *Political Research Quarterly*, Vol. 57, No. 2, June 2004, pp. 305–314.

Public Law 77-554, "An Act to Establish a Women's Army Auxiliary Corps for Service with the Army of the United States," May 14, 1942.

Ramsberger, Peter, Janice Laurence, and D. E. Sipes, "Retrospective Survey of Socialization, Values, and Performance in Relation to Recruit Training," in U.S. Congressional Commission on Military Training and Gender-Related Issues, *Congressional Commission on Military Training and Gender-Related Issues*, Vol. 4, Washington, D.C.: U.S. Government Printing Office, July 1999.

Rich, Motoko, "Old Tactic Gets New Use: Public Schools Separate Girls and Boys," *New York Times*, November 30, 2014.

Richman, Laura Smart, Michelle vanDellen, and Wendy Wood, "How Women Cope: Being a Numerical Minority in a Male-Dominated Profession," *Journal of Social Issues*, Vol. 67, No. 3, September 2011, pp. 492-509.

Riordan, C., *Girls and Boys in School: Together or Separate?* New York: Teachers College Press, 1990.

Rix, Sarah E., ed., *The American Woman 1990–1991: A Status Report for The Women's Research and Education Institute*, New York: W. W. Norton and Company, 1990.

Rosen, Leora N., Doris Durand, Paul Bliese, Ronald Halverson, Joseph Rothenberg, and Nancy Harrison, "Cohesion and Readiness in Gender-Integrated Combat Service Support Units: The Impact of Acceptance of Women and Gender Ratio," *Armed Forces and Society*, Vol. 22, No. 4, Summer 1996, pp. 537–553.

Rosen, Leora N., and Lee Martin, "Sexual Harassment, Cohesion, and Combat Readiness in U.S. Army Support Units," *Armed Forces and Society*, Vol. 24, No. 2, Winter 1998, pp. 221–244.

Rostker, Bernard, *I Want You! The Evolution of the All-Volunteer Force*, Santa Monica, Calif.: RAND Corporation, MG-265-RC, 2006. As of January 3, 2017: http://www.rand.org/pubs/monographs/MG265.html

Royse, David, Bruce A. Thyer, and Deborah K. Padgett, *Program Evaluation: An Introduction to an Evidence-Based Approach*, 6th ed., Boston: Cengage Learning, 2015.

RSMeans, *RSMeans Square Foot Costs*, 36th ed., Kingston, Mass., 2015.

Sabatier, Paul, "Top-Down and Bottom-Up Approaches to Implementation Research: a Critical Analysis and Suggested Synthesis," *Journal of Public Policy*, Vol. 6, 1986, pp. 21–48.

Sasson-Levy, Orna, and Sarit Amram-Katz, "Gender Integration in Israeli Officer Training: Degendering and Regendering the Military," *Signs*, Vol. 33, No. 1, 2007, pp. 105–133.

Scarpate, Jerry C., and Mary Anne O'Neill, "Evaluation of Gender Integration at Recruit Training Command," Defense Equal Opportunity Management Institute, July 1992.

Schaefer, Agnes Gereben, Jennie W. Wenger, Jennifer Kavanagh, Jonathan P. Wong, Gillian S. Oak, Thomas E. Trail, and Todd Nichols, *Implications of Integrating Women into the Marine Corps Infantry*, Santa Monica, Calif.: RAND Corporation, RR-1103-USMC, 2015. As of January 3, 2017: http://www.rand.org/pubs/research_reports/RR1103.html

Sekaquaptewa, Denise, and Mischa Thompson, "Solo Status, Stereotype Threat, and Performance Expectancies: Their Effects on Women's Performance," *Journal of Experimental Social Psychology*, Vol. 39, 2003, pp. 68–74.

Shadley, Robert D., *The GAMe: Unraveling a Military Sex Scandal*, Edina, Minn.: Beaver's Pond Press, 2013.

Simutis, Zita M., and Jacqueline A. Mottern, "Basic Combat Training in a Gender-Integrated Environment," briefing for Assistant Secretary of the Army (Manpower and Reserve Affairs), January 25, 1996.

Snyder, R. Claire, *Citizen-Soldiers and Manly Warriors: Military Service and Gender in the Civic Republican Tradition*, Lanham, Md.: Rowman and Littlefield, 1999.

Stiehm, Judith H., *Arms and the Enlisted Woman*, Philadelphia: Temple University Press, 1989.

Swim, J. K., and L. L. Cohen, "Overt, Covert, and Subtle Sexism: A Comparison Between the Attitudes Toward Women and Modern Sexism Scales," *Psychology of Women Quarterly*, 1997, pp. 21, 103–118.

Swim, K. J., Aikin, W. S. Hall, and B. A. Hunter, "Sexism and Racism: Old-Fashioned and Modern Prejudices," *Journal of Personality and Social Psychology*, 1995, pp. 199–214.

Torchia, Mariateresa, Andrea Clabro, and Morten Huse, "Women Directors on Corporate Boards: From Tokenism to Critical Mass," *Journal of Business Ethics*, Vol. 102, 2011, pp. 299-317.

"U.S. Air Force Almanac 2017," *Air Force Magazine*, June 2017, p. 42.

U.S. Air Force Air Education and Training Command, briefing, undated.

———, data set, May 2016. Not available to general public.

U.S. Congressional Commission on Military Training and Gender-Related Issues, *Congressional Commission on Military Training and Gender-Related Issues*, Vol. 2, Washington, D.C.: U.S. Government Printing Office, July 1999.

U.S. Department of the Air Force, *Air Force Response to the Report of the Federal Advisory Committee on Gender-Integrated Training*, Washington, D.C., May 28, 1999.

———, *Air Force Policy Directive 36-70: Diversity*, October 13, 2010.

U.S. Department of the Navy, Office of the Chief of Naval Operations, *OPNAV Instruction 1300.17B: Assignment of Women in the Navy*, Washington, D.C., May 27, 2011.

———, "Marine Corps Order 1510.32F: Recruit Training," Washington, D.C., December 20, 2012.

U.S. General Accounting Office, "Women in the Military: Deployment in the Persian Gulf War," report to the Secretary of Defense, Washington, D.C., July 1993.

———, "Basic Training: Services Are Using a Variety of Approaches to Gender Integration," report to the Chairman, Subcommittee on Military Personnel, Committee on National Security, House of Representatives, Washington, D.C., June 1996.

———, "Gender Issues: Perceptions of Readiness in Selected Units," report to the Ranking Minority Member, Subcommittee on Readiness and Management Support, Committee on Armed Services, U.S. Senate, Washington, D.C., May 1999.

U.S. House of Representatives Committee on Armed Services, "A Review of Sexual Misconduct by Basic Training Instructors at Lackland Air Force Base," hearing, 113th Congress, first session, January 23, 2013.

U.S. Marine Corps, "Depot Order 1513.6E: Recruit Training Order," 2014.

U.S. Marine Corps Operational Test and Evaluation Activity, *Ground Combat Element Integrated Task Force Experimental Assessment Report*, August 2015.

U.S. Navy Recruit Command, "Navy Recruiting Facts and Statistics," February 14, 2016. As of January 3, 2017:
http://www.cnrc.navy.mil/pages-nrc-links/nrc-facts-stats.htm.

Vecchio, Robert P., and Donna M. Brazil, "Leadership and Sex-Similarity: A Comparison in a Military Setting," *Personnel Psychology*, Vol. 60, No. 2, 2007, pp. 303–335.

W. K. Kellogg Foundation, "W. K. Kellogg Foundation Logic Model Development Guide," February 2, 2006.

Wong, Kristina, "Pentagon Pushes Female Troops Closer to Battlefield," *Washington Times*, May 14, 2012.

Yoder, Janice, "Rethinking Tokenism: Looking Beyond Numbers," *Gender and Society*, Vol. 5, No. 2, June 1991, pp. 178–192.

Zimmer, Lynn, "Tokenism and Women in the Workplace: The Limits of Gender-Neutral Theory," *Social Problems*, Vol. 35, No. 1, February 1988, pp. 64–77.